Captain Brassbound's Conversion

By George Bernard Shaw

A Digireads.com Book
Digireads.com Publishing

Captain Brassbound's Conversion
By George Bernard Shaw
ISBN: 1-4209-3289-6

This edition copyright © 2009

Please visit *www.digireads.com*

CAPTAIN BRASSBOUND'S CONVERSION

By George Bernard Shaw

ACT I

On the heights overlooking the harbor of Mogador, a seaport on the west coast of Morocco, the missionary, in the coolness of the late afternoon, is following the precept of Voltaire by cultivating his garden. He is an elderly Scotchman, spiritually a little weatherbeaten, as having to navigate his creed in strange waters crowded with other craft but still a convinced son of the Free Church and the North African Mission, with a faithful brown eye, and a peaceful soul. Physically a wiry small-knit man, well tanned, clean shaven, with delicate resolute features and a twinkle of mild humor. He wears the sun helmet and pagri, the neutral-tinted spectacles, and the white canvas Spanish sand shoes of the modern Scotch missionary: but instead of a cheap tourist's suit from Glasgow, a grey flannel shirt with white collar, a green sailor knot tie with a cheap pin in it, he wears a suit of clean white linen, acceptable in color, if not in cut, to the Moorish mind.

The view from the garden includes much Atlantic Ocean and a long stretch of sandy coast to the south, swept by the north east trade wind, and scantily nourishing a few stunted pepper trees, mangy palms, and tamarisks. The prospect ends, as far as the land is concerned, in little hills that come nearly to the sea: rudiments, these, of the Atlas Mountains. The missionary, having had daily opportunities of looking at this seascape for thirty years or so, pays no heed to it, being absorbed in trimming a huge red geranium bush, to English eyes unnaturally big, which, with a dusty smilax or two, is the sole product of his pet flower-bed. He is sitting to his work on a Moorish stool. In the middle of the garden there is a pleasant seat in the shade of a tamarisk tree. The house is in the south west corner of the garden, and the geranium bush in the north east corner.

At the garden-door of the house there appears presently a man who is clearly no barbarian, being in fact a less agreeable product peculiar to modern commercial civilization. His frame and flesh are those of an ill-nourished lad of seventeen; but his age is inscrutable: only the absence of any sign of grey in his mud colored hair suggests that he is at all events probably under forty, without prejudice to the possibility of his being under twenty. A Londoner would recognize him at once as an extreme but hardy specimen of the abortion produced by nature in a city slum. His utterance, affectedly pumped and hearty, and naturally vulgar and nasal, is ready and fluent: nature, a Board School education, and some kerbstone practice having made him a bit of an orator. His dialect, apart from its base nasal delivery, is not unlike that of smart London society in its tendency to replace diphthongs by vowels (sometimes rather prettily) and to shuffle all the traditional vowel pronunciations. He pronounces ow as ah, and i as aw, using the ordinary ow for o, i for ā, ă for ŭ, and ĕ for ă, with this reservation, that when any vowel is followed by an r he signifies its presence, not by pronouncing the r, which he never does under these circumstances, but by prolonging and modifyinq the vowel, sometimes even to the extreme degree of pronouncing it properly. As to his yol for l (a compendious delivery of the provincial eh-al), and other metropolitan refinements, amazing to all but cockneys, they cannot be indicated, save in the above imperfect manner, without the aid of a phonetic alphabet. He is dressed in somebody else's very second best as a coast-guardsman, and gives himself the airs of a stage tar with sufficient success to pass as a possible fish porter of bad character in casual employment during busy times at Billingsgate. His manner shows an earnest disposition to ingratiate himself with the missionary, probably for some dishonest purpose.

THE MAN. Awtenoon, Mr. Renkin. [*The missionary sits up quickly, and turns, resigning himself dutifully to the interruption.*] Yr honor's eolth.

RANKIN [*reservedly*]. Good afternoon, Mr. Drinkwotter.

DRINKWATER. You're not best pleased to be hinterrapted in yr bit o gawdnin bow the lawk o me, gavner.

RANKIN. A missionary knows nothing of leks of that soart, or of disleks either, Mr. Drinkwotter. What can I do for ye?

DRINKWATER [*heartily*]. Nathink, gavner. Awve brort noos fer yer.

RANKIN. Well, sit ye doon.

DRINKWATER. Aw thenk yr honor. [*He sits down on the seat under the tree and composes himself for conversation.*] Hever ear o Jadge Ellam?

RANKIN. Sir Howrrd Hallam?

DRINKWATER. Thet's im—enginest jadge in Hingland!—awlus gives the ket wen it's robbry with voylence, bless is awt. Aw sy nathink agin im: awm all fer lor mawseolf, aw em.

RANKIN. Well?

DRINKWATER. Hever ear of is sist-in-lor: Lidy Sisly Winefleet?

RANKIN. Do ye mean the celebrated Leddy—the traveller?

DRINKWATER. Yuss: should think aw doo. Walked acrost Harfricar with nathink but a little dawg, and wrowt abaht it in the Dily Mile (*the Daily Mail, a popular London newspaper*), she did.

RANKIN. Is she Sir Howrrd Hallam's sister-in-law?

DRINKWATER. Deeceased wawfe's sister: yuss: thet's wot she is.

RANKIN. Well, what about them?

DRINKWATER. Wot abaht them! Waw, they're eah. Lannid aht of a steam yacht in Mogador awber not twenty minnits agow. Gorn to the British cornsl's. E'll send em orn to you: *e* ynt got naowheres to put em. Sor em awr (*hire*) a Harab an two Krooboys to kerry their laggige. Thort awd cam an teoll yer.

RANKIN. Thank you. It's verra kind of you, Mr. Drinkwotter.

DRINKWATER. Down't mention it, gavner. Lor bless yer, wawn't it you as converted me? Wot was aw wen aw cam eah but a pore lorst sinner? Down't aw ow y'a turn fer thet? Besawds, gavner, this Lidy Sisly Winefleet mawt wor't to tike a walk crost Morocker—a rawd inter the mahntns or sech lawk. Weoll, as you knaow, gavner, thet cawn't be done eah withaht a hescort.

RANKIN. It's impoassible: th' would oall b' murrdered. Morocco is not lek the rest of Africa.

DRINKWATER. No, gavner: these eah Moors ez their religion; an it mikes em dinegerous. Hever convert a Moor, gavner?

RANKIN [*with a rueful smile*]. No.

DRINKWATER [*solemnly*]. Nor never will, gavner.

RANKIN. I have been at work here for twenty-five years, Mr. Drinkwotter; and you are my first and only convert.

DRINKWATER. Down't seem naow good, do it, gavner?

RANKIN. I don't say that. I hope I have done some good. They come to me for medicine when they are ill; and they call me the Christian who is not a thief. That is something.

DRINKWATER. Their mawnds kennot rawse to Christiennity lawk hahrs ken, gavner: thet's ah it is. Weoll, ez haw was syin, if a hescort is wornted, there's maw friend and commawnder Kepn Brarsbahnd of the schooner Thenksgivin, an is crew, incloodin mawseolf, will see the lidy an Jadge Ellam through henny little excursion in reason. Yr honor mawt mention it.

RANKIN. I will certainly not propose anything so dangerous as an excursion.

DRINKWATER [*virtuously*]. Naow, gavner, nor would I awst you to. [*Shaking his head.*] Naow, naow: it IS dinegerous. But hall the more call for a hescort if they should ev it hin their mawnds to gow.

RANKIN. I hope they won't.

DRINKWATER. An sow aw do too, gavner.

RANKIN [*pondering*]. 'Tis strange that they should come to Mogador, of all places; and to my house! I once met Sir Howrrd Hallam, years ago.

DRINKWATER [*amazed*]. Naow! didger? Think o thet, gavner! Waw, sow aw did too. But it were a misunnerstedin, thet wors. Lef the court withaht a stine on maw kerrickter, aw did.

RANKIN [*with some indignation*]. I hope you don't think I met Sir Howrrd in that way.

DRINKWATER. Mawt yeppn to the honestest, best meanin pusson, aw do assure yer, gavner.

RANKIN. I would have you to know that I met him privately, Mr. Drinkwotter. His brother was a dear friend of mine. Years ago. He went out to the West Indies.

DRINKWATER. The Wust Hindies! Jist acrost there, tather sawd thet howcean [*pointing seaward*]! Dear me! We cams hin with vennity, an we deepawts in dawkness. Down't we, gavner?

RANKIN [*pricking up his ears*]. Eh? Have you been reading that little book I gave you?

DRINKWATER. Aw hev, et odd tawms. Very camfitn, gavner. [*He rises, apprehensive lest further catechism should find him unprepared.*] Awll sy good awtenoon, gavner: you're busy hexpectin o Sr Ahrd an Lidy Sisly, ynt yer? [*About to go.*]

RANKIN [*stopping him*]. No, stop: we're oalways ready for travellers here. I have something else to say—a question to ask you.

DRINKWATER [*with a misgiving, which he masks by exaggerating his hearty sailor manner*]. An weollcome, yr honor.

RANKIN. Who is this Captain Brassbound?

DRINKWATER [*guiltily*]. Kepn Brarsbahnd! E's-weoll, e's maw Kepn, gavner.

RANKIN. Yes. Well?

DRINKWATER [*feebly*]. Kepn of the schooner Thenksgivin, gavner.

RANKIN [*searchingly*]. Have ye ever haird of a bad character in these seas called Black Paquito?

DRINKWATER [*with a sudden radiance of complete enlightenment*]. Aoh, nar aw tikes yer wiv me, yr honor. Nah sammun es bin a teolln you thet Kepn Brarsbahnd an Bleck Pakeetow is hawdentically the sime pussn. Ynt thet sow?

RANKIN. That is so. [D*rinkwater slaps his knee triumphantly. The missionary proceeds determinedly*] And the someone was a verra honest, straightforward man, as far as I could judge.

DRINKWATER [*embracing the implication*]. Course a wors, gavner: Ev aw said a word agin him? Ev aw nah?

RANKIN. But is Captain Brassbound Black Paquito then?

DRINKWATER. Waw, it's the nime is blessed mather give im at er knee, bless is little awt! Ther ynt naow awm in it. She ware a Wust Hinjin—howver there again, yer see [*pointing seaward*]—leastwaws, naow she worn't: she were a Brazilian, aw think; an Pakeetow's Brazilian for a bloomin little perrit—awskin yr pawdn for the word. [*Sentimentally*] Lawk as a Hinglish lidy mawt call er little boy Birdie.

RANKIN [*not quite convinced*]. But why Black Paquito?

DRINKWATER [*artlessly*]. Waw, the bird in its netral stite bein green, an e evin bleck air, y' knaow—

RANKIN [*cutting him short*]. I see. And now I will put ye another question. What is Captain Brassbound, or Paquito, or whatever he calls himself?

DRINKWATER [*officiously*]. Brarsbahnd, gavner. Awlus calls isseolf Brarsbahnd.

RANKIN. Well. Brassbound, then. What is he?

DRINKWATER [*fervently*]. You awks me wot e is, gavner?

RANKIN [*firmly*]. I do.

DRINKWATER [*with rising enthusiasm*]. An shll aw teoll yer wot e is, yr honor?

RANKIN [*not at all impressed*]. If ye will be so good, Mr. Drinkwotter.

DRINKWATER [*with overwhelming conviction*]. Then awll teoll you, gavner, wot he is. Ee's a Paffick Genlmn: thet's wot e is.

RANKIN [*gravely*]. Mr. Drinkwotter: pairfection is an attribute, not of West Coast captains, but of thr Maaker. And there are gentlemen and gentlemen in the world, espaecially in these latitudes. Which sort of gentleman is he?

DRINKWATER. Hinglish genlmn, gavner. Hinglish speakin; Hinglish fawther; West Hinjin plawnter; Hinglish true blue breed. [*Reflectively*] Tech o brahn from the mather, preps, she bein Brazilian.

RANKIN. Now on your faith as a Christian, Felix Drinkwotter, is Captain Brassbound a slaver or not?

DRINKWATER [*surprised into his natural cockney pertness*]. Naow e ynt.

RANKIN. Are ye sure?

DRINKWATER. Waw, a sliver is abaht the wanne thing in the wy of a genlmn o fortn thet e YNT.

RANKIN. I've haird that expression "gentleman of fortune" before, Mr. Drinkwotter. It means pirate. Do ye know that?

DRINKWATER. Bless y'r awt, y' cawnt be a pawrit naradys. Waw, the aw seas is wuss pleest nor Piccadilly Suckus. If aw was to do orn thet there Hetlentic Howcean the things aw did as a bwoy in the Worterleoo Rowd, awd ev maw air cat afore aw could turn maw ed. Pawrit be blaowed!—awskink yr pawdn, gavner. Nah, jest to shaow you ah little thet there striteforard man y' mide mention on knaowed wot e was atorkin abaht: oo would you spowse was the marster to wich Kepn Brarsbahnd served apprentice, as yr mawt sy?

RANKIN. I don't know.

DRINKWATER. Gawdn, gavner, Gawdn. Gawdn o Kawtoom—stetcher stends in Trifawlgr Square to this dy. Trined Bleck Pakeetow in smawshin hap the slive riders, e did. Promist Gawdn e wouldn't never smaggle slives nor gin, an [*with suppressed aggravation*] wownt, gavner, not if we gows dahn on ahr bloomin bended knees to im to do it.

RANKIN [*drily*]. And do ye go down on your bended knees to him to do it?

DRINKWATER [*somewhat abashed*]. Some of huz is hanconverted men, gavner; an they sy: You smaggles wanne thing, Kepn; waw not hanather?

RANKIN. We've come to it at last. I thought so. Captain Brassbound is a smuggler.

DRINKWATER. Weoll, waw not? Waw not, gavner? Ahrs is a Free Tride nition. It gows agin us as Hinglishmen to see these bloomin furriners settin ap their Castoms Ahses and spheres o hinfluence and sich lawk hall owver Arfricar. Daown't Harfricar belong as much to huz as to them? thet's wot we sy. Ennywys, there ynt naow awm in ahr business. All we daz is hescort, tourist hor commercial. Cook's hexcursions to the Hatlas Mahntns: thet's hall it is. Waw, it's spreadin civlawzytion, it is. Ynt it nah?

RANKIN. You think Captain Brassbound's crew sufficiently equipped for that, do you?

DRINKWATER. Hee-quipped! Haw should think sow. Lawtnin rawfles, twelve shots in the meggezine! Oo's to storp us?

RANKIN. The most dangerous chieftain in these parts, the Sheikh Sidi el Assif, has a new American machine pistol which fires ten bullets without loadin; and his rifle has sixteen shots in the magazine.

DRINKWATER [*indignantly*]. Yuss; an the people that sells sich things into the ends o' them eathen bleck niggers calls theirseolves Christians! It's a crool shime, sow it is.

RANKIN. If a man has the heart to pull the trigger, it matters little what color his hand is, Mr. Drinkwotter. Have ye anything else to say to me this afternoon?

DRINKWATER [*rising*]. Nathink, gavner, cept to wishyer the bust o yolth, and a many cornverts. Awtenoon, gavner.

RANKIN. Good afternoon to ye, Mr. Drinkwotter.

[*As Drinkwater turns to go, a Moorish porter comes from the house with two Krooboys.*]

THE PORTER [*at the door, addressing Rankin*]. Bikouros [*Moroccan for Epicurus, a general Moorish name for the missionaries, who are supposed by the Moors to have chosen their calling through a love of luxurious idleness*]: I have brought to your house a Christian dog and his woman.

DRINKWATER. There's eathen menners fer yer! Calls Sr Ahrd Ellam an Lidy Winefleet a Christian dorg and is woman! If ee ed you in the dorck et the Centl Crimnal, you'd fawnd aht oo was the dorg and oo was is marster, pretty quick, you would.

RANKIN. Have you broat their boxes?

THE PORTER. By Allah, two camel loads!

RANKIN. Have you been paid?

THE PORTER. Only one miserable dollar, Bikouros. I have brought them to your house. They will pay you. Give me something for bringing gold to your door.

DRINKWATER. Yah! You oughter bin bawn a Christian, you ought. You knaow too mach.

RANKIN. You have broat onnly trouble and expense to my door, Hassan; and you know it. Have I ever charged your wife and children for my medicines?

HASSAN [*philosophically*]. It is always permitted by the Prophet to ask, Bikouros. [*He goes cheerfully into the house with the Krooboys.*]

DRINKWATER. Jist thort eed trah it orn, a did. Hooman nitre is the sime everywheres. Them eathens is jast lawk you an' me, gavner.

[*A lady and gentleman, both English, come into the garden. The gentleman, more than elderly, is facing old age on compulsion, not resignedly. He is clean shaven, and has a brainy rectangular forehead, a resolute nose with strongly governed nostrils, and a tightly fastened down mouth which has evidently shut in much temper and anger in its time. He has a habit of deliberately assumed authority and dignity, but is trying to take life more genially and easily in his character of tourist, which is further borne out by his white hat and summery racecourse attire.*

The lady is between thirty and forty, tall, very good-looking, sympathetic, intelligent, tender and humorous, dressed with cunning simplicity not as a businesslike, tailor made, gaitered tourist, but as if she lived at the next cottage and had dropped in for tea in blouse and flowered straw hat. A woman of great vitality and humanity, who begins a casual acquaintance at the point usually attained by English people after thirty years acquaintance when they are capable of reaching it at all. She pounces genially on Drinkwater, who is smirking at her, hat in hand, with an air of hearty welcome. The gentleman, on the other hand, comes down the side of the garden next the house, instinctively maintaining a distance between himself and the others.]

THE LADY [*to Drinkwater*]. How dye do? Are you the missionary?

DRINKWATER [*modestly*]. Naow, lidy, aw will not deceive you, thow the mistike his but netral. Awm wanne of the missionary's good works, lidy—is first cornvert, a umble British seaman—countrymen o yours, lidy, and of is lawdship's. This eah is Mr. Renkin, the bust worker in the wust cowst vawnyawd. [*Introducing the judge*] Mr. Renkin: is lawdship Sr Ahrd Ellam. [*He withdraws discreetly into the house.*]

SIR HOWARD [*to Rankin*]. I am sorry to intrude on you, Mr. Rankin; but in the absence of a hotel there seems to be no alternative.

LADY CICELY [*beaming on him*]. Besides, we would so much rather stay with you, if you will have us, Mr. Rankin.

SIR HOWARD [*introducing her*]. My sister-in-law, Lady Cicely Waynflete, Mr. Rankin.

RANKIN. I am glad to be of service to your leddyship. You will be wishing to have some tea after your journey, I'm thinking.

LADY CICELY. Thoughtful man that you are, Mr. Rankin! But we've had some already on board the yacht. And I've arranged everything with your servants; so you must go on gardening just as if we were not here.

SIR HOWARD. I am sorry to have to warn you, Mr. Rankin, that Lady Cicely, from travelling in Africa, has acquired a habit of walking into people's houses and behaving as if she were in her own.

LADY CICELY. But, my dear Howard, I assure you the natives like it.

RANKIN [*gallantly*]. So do I.

LADY CICELY [*delighted*]. Oh, that is so nice of you, Mr. Rankin. This is a delicious country! And the people seem so good! They have such nice faces! We had such a handsome Moor to carry our luggage up! And two perfect pets of Krooboys! Did you notice their faces, Howard?

SIR HOWARD. I did; and I can confidently say, after a long experience of faces of the worst type looking at me from the dock, that I have never seen so entirely villainous a trio as that Moor and the two Krooboys, to whom you gave five dollars when they would have been perfectly satisfied with one.

RANKIN [*throwing up his hands*]. Five dollars! 'Tis easy to see you are not Scotch, my leddy.

LADY CICELY. Oh, poor things, they must want it more than we do; and you know, Howard, that Mahometans never spend money in drink.

RANKIN. Excuse me a moment, my leddy. I have a word in season to say to that same Moor. [*He goes into the house.*]

LADY CICELY [*walking about the garden, looking at the view and at the flowers*]. I think this is a perfectly heavenly place.

[*Drinkwater returns from the house with a chair.*]

DRINKWATER [*placing the chair for Sir Howard*]. Awskink yr pawdn for the libbety, Sr Ahrd.

SIR HOWARD [*looking a him*]. I have seen you before somewhere.

DRINKWATER. You ev, Sr Ahrd. But aw do assure yer it were hall a mistike.

SIR HOWARD. As usual. [*He sits down.*] Wrongfully convicted, of course.

DRINKWATER [*with sly delight*]. Naow, gavner. [*Half whispering, with an ineffable grin*] Wrorngfully hacquittid!

SIR HOWARD. Indeed! That's the first case of the kind I have ever met.

DRINKWATER. Lawd, Sr Ahrd, wot jagginses them jurymen was! You an me knaowed it too, didn't we?

SIR HOWARD. I daresay we did. I am sorry to say I forget the exact nature of the difficulty you were in. Can you refresh my memory?

DRINKWATER. Owny the aw sperrits o youth, y' lawdship. Worterleoo Rowd kice. Wot they calls Ooliganism.

SIR HOWARD. Oh! You were a Hooligan, were you?

LADY CICELY [*puzzled*]. A Hooligan!

DRINKWATER [*deprecatingly*]. Nime giv huz pore thortless leds baw a gent on the Dily Chrornicle, lidy. [*Rankin returns. Drinkwater immediately withdraws, stopping the missionary for a moment near the threshold to say, touching his forelock*] Awll eng abaht within ile, gavner, hin kice aw should be wornted. [*He goes into the house with soft steps.*]

[*Lady Cicely sits down on the bench under the tamarisk. Rankin takes his stool from the flowerbed and sits down on her left, Sir Howard being on her right.*]

LADY CICELY. What a pleasant face your sailor friend has, Mr. Rankin! He has been so frank and truthful with us. You know I don't think anybody can pay me a greater compliment than to be quite sincere with me at first sight. It's the perfection of natural good manners.

SIR HOWARD. You must not suppose, Mr. Rankin, that my sister-in-law talks nonsense on purpose. She will continue to believe in your friend until he steals her watch; and even then she will find excuses for him.

RANKIN [*drily changing the subject*]. And how have ye been, Sir Howrrd, since our last meeting that morning nigh forty year ago down at the docks in London?

SIR HOWARD [*greatly surprised, pulling himself together*] Our last meeting! Mr. Rankin: have I been unfortunate enough to forget an old acquaintance?

RANKIN. Well, perhaps hardly an acquaintance, Sir Howrrd. But I was a close friend of your brother Miles: and when he sailed for Brazil I was one of the little party that saw him off. You were one of the party also, if I'm not mistaken. I took particular notice of you because you were Miles's brother and I had never seen ye before. But ye had no call to take notice of me.

SIR HOWARD [*reflecting*]. Yes: there was a young friend of my brother's who might well be you. But the name, as I recollect it, was Leslie.

RANKIN. That was me, sir. My name is Leslie Rankin; and your brother and I were always Miles and Leslie to one another.

SIR HOWARD [*pluming himself a little*]. Ah! that explains it. I can trust my memory still, Mr. Rankin; though some people do complain that I am growing old.

RANKIN. And where may Miles be now, Sir Howard?

SIR HOWARD [*abruptly*]. Don't you know that he is dead?

RANKIN [*much shocked*]. Never haird of it. Dear, dear: I shall never see him again; and I can scarcely bring his face to mind after all these years. [*With moistening eyes, which at once touch Lady Cicely's sympathy*] I'm right sorry—right sorry.

SIR HOWARD [*decorously subduing his voice*]. Yes: he did not live long: indeed, he never came back to England. It must be nearly thirty years ago now that he died in the West Indies on his property there.

RANKIN [*surprised*]. His proaperty! Miles with a proaperty!

SIR HOWARD. Yes: he became a planter, and did well out there, Mr. Rankin. The history of that property is a very curious and interesting one—at least it is so to a lawyer like myself.

RANKIN. I should be glad to hear it for Miles's sake, though I am no lawyer, Sir Howrrd.

LADY CICELY. I never knew you had a brother, Howard.

SIR HOWARD [*not pleased by this remark*]. Perhaps because you never asked me. [*Turning more blandly to Rankin*] I will tell you the story, Mr. Rankin. When Miles died, he left an estate in one of the West Indian islands. It was in charge of an agent who was a sharpish fellow, with all his wits about him. Now, sir, that man did a thing which probably could hardly be done with impunity even here in Morocco, under the most barbarous of surviving civilizations. He quite simply took the estate for himself and kept it.

RANKIN. But how about the law?

SIR HOWARD. The law, sir, in that island, consisted practically of the Attorney General and the Solicitor General; and these gentlemen were both retained by the agent. Consequently there was no solicitor in the island to take up the case against him.

RANKIN. Is such a thing possible to-day in the British Empire?

SIR HOWARD [*calmly*]. Oh, quite. Quite.

LADY CICELY. But could not a first-rate solicitor have been sent out from London?

SIR HOWARD. No doubt, by paying him enough to compensate him for giving up his London practice: that is, rather more than there was any reasonable likelihood of the estate proving worth.

RANKIN. Then the estate was lost?

SIR HOWARD. Not permanently. It is in my hands at present.

RANKIN. Then how did ye get it back?

SIR HOWARD [*with crafty enjoyment of his own cunning*]. By hoisting the rogue with his own petard. I had to leave matters as they were for many years; for I had my own position in the world to make. But at last I made it. In the course of a holiday trip to the West Indies, I found that this dishonest agent had left the island, and placed the estate in the hands of an agent of his own, whom he was foolish enough to pay very badly. I put the case before that agent; and he decided to treat the estate as my property. The robber now found himself in exactly the same position he had formerly forced me into. Nobody in the island would act against me, least of all the Attorney and Solicitor General, who appreciated my influence at the Colonial Office. And so I got the estate back. "The mills of the gods grind slowly," Mr. Rankin; "but they grind exceeding small."

LADY CICELY. Now I suppose if I'd done such a clever thing in England, you'd have sent me to prison.

SIR HOWARD. Probably, unless you had taken care to keep outside the law against conspiracy. Whenever you wish to do anything against the law, Cicely, always consult a good solicitor first.

LADY CICELY. So I do. But suppose your agent takes it into his head to give the estate back to his wicked old employer!

SIR HOWARD. I heartily wish he would.

RANKIN [*openeyed*]. You wish he would!!

SIR HOWARD. Yes. A few years ago the collapse of the West Indian sugar industry converted the income of the estate into an annual loss of about £150 a year. If I can't sell it soon, I shall simply abandon it—unless you, Mr. Rankin, would like to take it as a present.

RANKIN [*laughing*]. I thank your lordship: we have estates enough of that sort in Scotland. You're setting with your back to the sun, Leddy Ceecily, and losing something worth looking at. See there. [*He rises and points seaward, where the rapid twilight of the latitude has begun.*]

LADY CICELY [*getting up to look and uttering a cry of admiration*]. Oh, how lovely!

SIR HOWARD [*also rising*]. What are those hills over there to the southeast?

RANKIN. They are the outposts, so to speak, of the Atlas Mountains.

LADY CICELY. The Atlas Mountains! Where Shelley's witch lived! We'll make an excursion to them to-morrow, Howard.

RANKIN. That's impossible, my leddy. The natives are verra dangerous.

LADY CICELY. Why? Has any explorer been shooting them?

RANKIN. No. But every man of them believes he will go to heaven if he kills an unbeliever.

LADY CICELY. Bless you, dear Mr. Rankin, the people in England believe that they will go to heaven if they give all their property to the poor. But they don't do it. I'm not a bit afraid of that.

RANKIN. But they are not accustomed to see women going about unveiled.

LADY CICELY. I always get on best with people when they can see my face.

SIR HOWARD. Cicely: you are talking great nonsense and you know it. These people have no laws to restrain them, which means, in plain English, that they are habitual thieves and murderers.

RANKIN. Nay, nay: not exactly that.

LADY CICELY [*indignantly*]. Of course not. You always think, Howard, that nothing prevents people killing each other but the fear of your hanging them for it. But what nonsense that is! And how wicked! If these people weren't here for some good purpose, they wouldn't have been made, would they, Mr. Rankin?

RANKIN. That is a point, certainly, Leddy Ceecily.

SIR HOWARD. Oh, if you are going to talk theology—

LADY CICELY. Well, why not? theology is as respectable as law, I should think. Besides, I'm only talking commonsense. Why do people get killed by savages? Because instead of being polite to them, and saying Howdyedo? like me, people aim pistols at them. I've been among savages—cannibals and all sorts. Everybody said they'd kill me. But when I met them, I said Howdyedo? and they were quite nice. The kings always wanted to marry me.

SIR HOWARD. That does not seem to me to make you any safer here, Cicely. You shall certainly not stir a step beyond the protection of the consul, if I can help it, without a strong escort.

LADY CICELY. I don't want an escort.

SIR HOWARD. I do. And I suppose you will expect me to accompany you.

RANKIN. 'Tis not safe, Leddy Ceecily. Really and truly, 'tis not safe. The tribes are verra fierce; and there are cities here that no Christian has ever set foot in. If you go without being well protected, the first chief you meet well seize you and send you back again to prevent his followers murdering you.

LADY CICELY. Oh, how nice of him, Mr. Rankin!

RANKIN. He would not do it for your sake, Leddy Ceecily, but for his own. The Sultan would get into trouble with England if you were killed; and the Sultan would kill the chief to pacify the English government.

LADY CICELY. But I always go everywhere. I know the people here won't touch me. They have such nice faces and such pretty scenery.

SIR HOWARD [*to Rankin, sitting down again resignedly*]. You can imagine how much use there is in talking to a woman who admires the faces of the ruffians who infest these ports, Mr. Rankin. Can anything be done in the way of an escort?

RANKIN. There is a certain Captain Brassbound here who trades along the coast, and occasionally escorts parties of merchants on journeys into the interior. I understand that he served under Gordon in the Soudan.

SIR HOWARD. That sounds promising. But I should like to know a little more about him before I trust myself in his hands.

RANKIN. I quite agree with you, Sir Howrrd. I'll send Felix Drinkwotter for him. [*He claps his hands. An Arab boy appears at the house door.*] Muley: is sailor man here? [*Muley nods.*] Tell sailor man bring captain. [*Muley nods and goes.*]

SIR HOWARD. Who is Drinkwater?

RANKIN. His agent, or mate: I don't rightly know which.

LADY CICELY. Oh, if he has a mate named Felix Drinkwater, it must be quite a respectable crew. It is such a nice name.

RANKIN. You saw him here just now. He is a convert of mine.

LADY CICELY [*delighted*]. That nice truthful sailor!

SIR HOWARD [*horrified*]. What! The Hooligan!

RANKIN [*puzzled*]. Hooligan? No, my lord: he is an Englishman.

SIR HOWARD. My dear Mr. Rankin, this man was tried before me on a charge of street ruffianism.

RANKIN. So he told me. He was badly broat up, I am afraid. But he is now a converted man.

LADY CICELY. Of course he is. His telling you so frankly proves it. You know, really, Howard, all those poor people whom you try are more sinned against than sinning. If you would only talk to them in a friendly way instead of passing cruel sentences on them, you would find them quite nice to you. [*Indignantly*] I won't have this poor man trampled on merely because his mother brought him up as a Hooligan. I am sure nobody could be nicer than he was when he spoke to us.

SIR HOWARD. In short, we are to have an escort of Hooligans commanded by a filibuster. Very well, very well. You will most likely admire all their faces; and I have no doubt at all that they will admire yours.

[*Drinkwater comes from the house with an Italian dressed in a much worn suit of blue serge, a dilapidated Alpine hat, and boots laced with scraps of twine. He remains near the door, whilst Drinkwater comes forward between Sir Howard and Lady Cicely.*]

DRINKWATER. Yr honor's servant. [*To the Italian*] Mawtzow: is lawdship Sr Ahrd Ellam. [*Marzo touches his hat.*] Er Lidyship Lidy Winefleet. [*Marzo touches his hat.*] Hawtellian shipmite, lidy. Hahr chef.

LADY CICELY [*nodding affably to Marzo*]. Howdyedo? I love Italy. What part of it were you born in?

DRINKWATER. Worn't bawn in Hitly at all, lidy. Bawn in Ettn Gawdn (Hatton Garden). Hawce barrer an street pianner Hawtellian, lidy: thet's wot e is. Kepn Brarsbahnd's respects to yr honors; an e awites yr commawnds.

RANKIN. Shall we go indoors to see him?

SIR HOWARD. I think we had better have a look at him by daylight.

RANKIN. Then we must lose no time: the dark is soon down in this latitude. [*To Drinkwater*] Will ye ask him to step out here to us, Mr. Drinkwotter?

DRINKWATER. Rawt you aw, gavner. [*He goes officiously into the house.*]

[*Lady Cicely and Rankin sit down as before to receive the Captain. The light is by this time waning rapidly, the darkness creeping west into the orange crimson.*]

LADY CICELY [*whispering*]. Don't you feel rather creepy, Mr. Rankin? I wonder what he'll be like.

RANKIN. I misdoubt me he will not answer, your leddyship.

[*There is a scuffling noise in the house; and Drinkwater shoots out through the doorway across the garden with every appearance of having been violently kicked. Marzo immediately hurries down the garden on Sir Howard's right out of the neighborhood of the doorway.*]

DRINKWATER [*trying to put a cheerful air on much mortification and bodily anguish*]. Narsty step to thet ere door tripped me hap, it did. [*Raising his voice and narrowly escaping a squeak of pain*] Kepn Brarsbahnd. [*He gets as far from the house as possible, on Rankin's left. Rankin rises to receive his guest.*]

[*An olive complexioned man with dark southern eyes and hair comes from the house. Age about 36. Handsome features, but joyless; dark eyebrows drawn towards one another; mouth set grimly; nostrils large and strained: a face set to one tragic purpose. A man of few words, fewer gestures, and much significance. On the whole, interesting, and even attractive, but not friendly. He stands for a moment, saturnine in the ruddy light, to see who is present, looking in a singular and rather deadly way at Sir Howard; then with some surprise and uneasiness at Lady Cicely. Finally he comes down into the middle of the garden, and confronts Rankin, who has been glaring at him in consternation from the moment of his entrance, and continues to do so in so marked a way that the glow in Brassbound's eyes deepens as he begins to take offence.*]

BRASSBOUND. Well, sir, have you stared your fill at me?

RANKIN [*recovering himself with a start*]. I ask your pardon for my bad manners, Captain Brassbound. Ye are extraordinair lek an auld college friend of mine, whose face I said not ten minutes gone that I could no longer bring to mind. It was as if he had come from the grave to remind me of it.

BRASSBOUND. Why have you sent for me?

RANKIN. We have a matter of business with ye, Captain.

BRASSBOUND. Who are "we"?

RANKIN. This is Sir Howrrd Hallam, who will be well known to ye as one of Her Majesty's judges.

BRASSBOUND [*turning the singular look again on Sir Howard*]. The friend of the widow! the protector of the fatherless!

SIR HOWARD [*startled*]. I did not know I was so favorably spoken of in these parts, Captain Brassbound. We want an escort for a trip into the mountains.

BRASSBOUND [*ignoring this announcement*]. Who is the lady?

RANKIN. Lady Ceecily Waynflete, his lordship's sister-in-law.

LADY CICELY. Howdyedo, Captain Brassbound? [He bows gravely.]

SIR HOWARD [*a little impatient of these questions, which strike him as somewhat impertinent*]. Let us come to business, if you please. We are thinking of making a short excursion to see the country about here. Can you provide us with an escort of respectable, trustworthy men?

BRASSBOUND. No.

DRINKWATER [*in strong remonstrance*]. Nah, nah, nah! Nah look eah, Kepn, y'knaow—

BRASSBOUND [*between his teeth*]. Hold your tongue.

DRINKWATER [*abjectly*]. Yuss, Kepn.

RANKIN. I understood it was your business to provide escorts, Captain Brassbound.

BRASSBOUND. You were rightly informed. That IS my business.

LADY CICELY. Then why won't you do it for us?

BRASSBOUND. You are not content with an escort. You want respectable, trustworthy men. You should have brought a division of London policemen with you. My men are neither respectable nor trustworthy.

DRINKWATER [*unable to contain himself*]. Nah, nah, look eah, Kepn. If you want to be moddist, be moddist on your aown accahnt, nort on mawn.

BRASSBOUND. You see what my men are like. That rascal [indicating Marzo] would cut a throat for a dollar if he had courage enough.

MARZO. I not understand. I no spik Englis.

BRASSBOUND. This thing [*pointing to Drinkwater*] is the greatest liar, thief, drunkard, and rapscallion on the west coast.

DRINKWATER [*affecting an ironic indifference*]. Gow orn, Gow orn. Sr Ahrd ez erd witnesses to maw kerrickter afoah. *E* knaows ah mech to believe of em.

LADY CICELY. Captain Brassbound: I have heard all that before about the blacks; and I found them very nice people when they were properly treated.

DRINKWATER [*chuckling: the Italian is also grinning*]. Nah, Kepn, nah! Owp yr prahd o y'seolf nah.

BRASSBOUND. I quite understand the proper treatment for him, madam. If he opens his mouth again without my leave, I will break every bone in his skin.

LADY CICELY [*in her most sunnily matter-of-fact way*]. Does Captain Brassbound always treat you like this, Mr. Drinkwater?

[*Drinkwater hesitates, and looks apprehensively at the Captain.*]

BRASSBOUND. Answer, you dog, when the lady orders you. [*To Lady Cicely*] Do not address him as Mr. Drinkwater, madam: he is accustomed to be called Brandyfaced Jack.

DRINKWATER [*indignantly*]. Eah, aw sy! nah look eah, Kepn: maw nime is Drinkworter. You awsk em et Sin Jorn's in the Worterleoo Rowd. Orn maw grenfawther's tombstown, it is.

BRASSBOUND. It will be on your own tombstone, presently, if you cannot hold your tongue. [*Turning to the others*] Let us understand one another, if you please. An escort here, or anywhere where there are no regular disciplined forces, is what its captain makes it. If I undertake this business, I shall be your escort. I may require a dozen men, just as I may require a dozen horses. Some of the horses will be vicious; so will all the men. If either horse or man tries any of his viciousness on me, so much the worse for him; but it will make no difference to you. I will order my men to behave themselves before the lady; and they shall obey their orders. But the lady will please understand that I take my own way with them and suffer no interference.

LADY CICELY. Captain Brassbound: I don't want an escort at all. It will simply get us all into danger; and I shall have the trouble of getting it out again. That's what escorts always do. But since Sir Howard prefers an escort, I think you had better stay at home and let me take charge of it. I know your men will get on perfectly well if they're properly treated.

DRINKWATER [*with enthusiasm*]. Feed aht o yr and, lidy, we would.

BRASSBOUND [*with sardonic assent*]. Good. I agree. [*To Drinkwater*] You shall go without me.

DRINKWATER. [*terrified*]. Eah! Wot are you a syin orn? We cawn't gow withaht yer. [*To Lady Cicely*] Naow, lidy: it wouldn't be for yr hown good. Yer cawn't hexpect a lot o poor honeddikited men lawk huz to ran ahrseolvs into dineger withaht naow Kepn to teoll us wot to do. Naow, lidy: hoonawted we stend: deevawdid we fall.

LADY CICELY. Oh, if you prefer your captain, have him by all means. Do you like to be treated as he treats you?

DRINKWATER [*with a smile of vanity*]. Weoll, lidy: y cawn't deenaw that e's a Paffick Genlmn. Bit hawbitrairy, preps; but hin a genlmn you looks for sich. It tikes a hawbitrairy wanne to knock aht them eathen Shikes, aw teoll yer.

BRASSBOUND. That's enough. Go.

DRINKWATER. Weoll, aw was hownly a teolln the lidy thet— [*A threatening movement from Brassbound cuts him short. He flies for his life into the house, followed by the Italian.*]

BRASSBOUND. Your ladyship sees. These men serve me by their own free choice. If they are dissatisfied, they go. If I am dissatisfied, they go. They take care that I am not dissatisfied.

SIR HOWARD [*who has listened with approval and growing confidence*]. Captain Brassbound: you are the man I want. If your terms are at all reasonable, I will accept your services if we decide to make an excursion. You do not object, Cicely, I hope.

LADY CICELY. Oh no. After all, those men must really like you, Captain Brassbound. I feel sure you have a kind heart. You have such nice eyes.

SIR HOWARD [*scandalized*]. My dear Cicely: you really must restrain your expressions of confidence in people's eyes and faces. [*To Brassbound*] Now, about terms, Captain?

BRASSBOUND. Where do you propose to go?

SIR HOWARD. I hardly know. Where can we go, Mr. Rankin?

RANKIN. Take my advice, Sir Howrrd. Don't go far.

BRASSBOUND. I can take you to Meskala, from which you can see the Atlas Mountains. From Meskala I can take you to an ancient castle in the hills, where you can put up as long as you please. The customary charge is half a dollar a man per day and his food. *I* charge double.

SIR HOWARD. I suppose you answer for your men being sturdy fellows, who will stand to their guns if necessary.

BRASSBOUND. I can answer for their being more afraid of me than of the Moors.

LADY CICELY. That doesn't matter in the least, Howard. The important thing, Captain Brassbound, is: first, that we should have as few men as possible, because men give such a lot of trouble travelling. And then, they must have good lungs and not be always catching cold. Above all, their clothes must be of good wearing material. Otherwise I shall be nursing and stitching and mending all the way; and it will be trouble enough, I assure you, to keep them washed and fed without that.

BRASSBOUND [*haughtily*]. My men, madam, are not children in the nursery.

LADY CICELY [*with unanswerable conviction*]. Captain Brassbound: all men are children in the nursery. I see that you don't notice things. That poor Italian had only one proper bootlace: the other was a bit of string. And I am sure from Mr. Drinkwater's complexion that he ought to have some medicine.

BRASSBOUND [*outwardly determined not to be trifled with: inwardly puzzled and rather daunted*]. Madam: if you want an escort, I can provide you with an escort. If you want a Sunday School treat, I can not provide it.

LADY CICELY [*with sweet melancholy*]. Ah, don't you wish you could, Captain? Oh, if I could only show you my children from Waynflete Sunday School! The darlings would love this place, with all the camels and black men. I'm sure you would enjoy having them here, Captain Brassbound; and it would be such an education for your men! [*Brassbound stares at her with drying lips.*]

SIR HOWARD. Cicely: when you have quite done talking nonsense to Captain Brassbound, we can proceed to make some definite arrangement with him.

LADY CICELY. But it's arranged already. We'll start at eight o'clock to-morrow morning, if you please, Captain. Never mind about the Italian: I have a big box of clothes with me for my brother in Rome; and there are some bootlaces in it. Now go home to bed and don't fuss yourself. All you have to do is to bring your men round; and I'll see to the rest. Men are always so nervous about moving. Goodnight. [*She offers him her hand. Surprised, he pulls off his cap for the first time. Some scruple prevents him from taking her hand at once. He hesitates; then turns to Sir Howard and addresses him with warning earnestness.*]

BRASSBOUND. Sir Howard Hallam: I advise you not to attempt this expedition.

SIR HOWARD. Indeed! Why?

BRASSBOUND. You are safe here. I warn you, in those hills there is a justice that is not the justice of your courts in England. If you have wronged a man, you may meet that man there. If you have wronged a woman, you may meet her son there. The justice of those hills is the justice of vengeance.

SIR HOWARD [*faintly amused*]. You are superstitious, Captain. Most sailors are, I notice. However, I have complete confidence in your escort.

BRASSBOUND [*almost threateningly*]. Take care. The avenger may be one of the escort.

SIR HOWARD. I have already met the only member of your escort who might have borne a grudge against me, Captain; and he was acquitted.

BRASSBOUND. You are fated to come, then?

SIR HOWARD [*smiling*]. It seems so.

BRASSBOUND. On your head be it! [*To Lady Cicely, accepting her hand at last*] Goodnight.

[*He goes. It is by this time starry night.*]

ACT II

Midday. A roam in a Moorish castle. A divan seat runs round the dilapidated adobe walls, which are partly painted, partly faced with white tiles patterned in green and yellow. The ceiling is made up of little squares, painted in bright colors, with gilded edges, and ornamented with gilt knobs. On the cement floor are mattings, sheepskins, and leathern cushions with geometrical patterns on them. There is a tiny Moorish table in the middle; and at it a huge saddle, with saddle cloths of various colors, showing that the room is used by foreigners accustomed to chairs. Anyone sitting at the table in this seat would have the chief entrance, a large horseshoe arch, on his left, and another saddle seat between him and the arch; whilst, if susceptible to draughts, he would probably catch cold from a little Moorish door in the wall behind him to his right.

Two or three of Brassbound's men, overcome by the midday heat, sprawl supine on the floor, with their reefer coats under their heads, their knees uplifted, and their calves laid comfortably on the divan. Those who wear shirts have them open at the throat for greater coolness. Some have jerseys. All wear boots and belts, and have guns ready to their hands. One of them, lying with his head against the second saddle seat, wears what was once a fashionable white English yachting suit. He is evidently a pleasantly worthless young English gentleman gone to the bad, but retaining sufficient self-respect to shave carefully and brush his hair, which is wearing thin, and does not seem to have been luxuriant even in its best days.

The silence is broken only by the snores of the young gentleman, whose mouth has fallen open, until a few distant shots half waken him. He shuts his mouth convulsively, and opens his eyes sleepily. A door is violently kicked outside; and the voice of Drinkwater is heard raising urgent alarm.

DRINKWATER. Wot ow! Wike ap there, will yr. Wike ap. [*He rushes in through the horseshoe arch, hot and excited, and runs round, kicking the sleepers*] Nah then. Git ap. Git ap, will yr, Kiddy Redbrook. [*He gives the young gentleman a rude shove.*]

REDBOOK [*sitting up*]. Stow that, will you. What's amiss?

DRINKWATER [*disgusted*]. Wot's amiss! Didn't eah naow fawrin, I spowse.

REDBROOK. No.

DRINKWATER [*sneering*]. Naow. Thort it sifer nort, didn't yr?

REDBROOK [*with crisp intelligence*]. What! You're running away, are you? [*He springs up, crying*] Look alive, Johnnies: there's danger. Brandyfaced Jack's on the run. [*They spring up hastily, grasping their guns.*]

DRINKWATER. Dineger! Yuss: should think there wors dineger. It's howver, thow, as it mowstly his baw the tawm you're awike. [*They relapse into lassitude.*] Waw wasn't you on the look-aht to give us a end? Bin hattecked baw the Benny Seeras (*Beni Siras*), we ev, an ed to rawd for it pretty strite, too, aw teoll yr. Mawtzow is it: the bullet glawnst all rahnd is bloomin brisket. Brarsbahnd e dropt the Shike's oss at six unnern fifty yawds. [*Bustling them about*] Nah then: git the plice ready for the British herristoracy, Lawd Ellam and Lidy Wineflete.

REDBOOK. Lady faint, eh?

DRINKWATER. Fynt! Not lawkly. Wornted to gow an talk, to the Benny Seeras: blaow me if she didn't! huz wot we was frahtnd of. Tyin up Mawtzow's wound, she is, like a bloomin orspittle nass. [*Sir Howard, with a copious pagri on his white hat, enters through the horseshoe arch, followed by a couple of men supporting the wounded Marzo, who, weeping and terrorstricken by the prospect of death and of subsequent torments for which he is conscious of having eminently qualified himself, has his coat off and a bandage round his chest. One of his supporters is a black-bearded, thickset, slow, middle-aged man with an air of damaged respectability, named—as it afterwards appears—Johnson. Lady Cicely walks beside Marzo. Redbrook, a little shamefaced, crosses the room to the opposite wall as far away as possible from the visitors. Drinkwater turns and receives them with jocular ceremony.*] Weolcome to Brarsbahnd Cawstl, Sr Ahrd an lidy. This eah is the corfee and commercial room.

[*Sir Howard goes to the table and sits on the saddle, rather exhausted. Lady Cicely comes to Drinkwater.*]

LADY CICELY. Where is Marzo's bed?

DRINKWATER. Is bed, lidy? Weoll: e ynt petickler, lidy. E ez is chawce of henny flegstown agin thet wall.

[*They deposit Marzo on the flags against the wall close to the little door. He groans. Johnson phlegmatically leaves him and joins Redbrook.*]

LADY CICELY. But you can't leave him there in that state.

DRINKWATER. Ow: e's hall rawt. [*Strolling up callously to Marzo*] You're hall rawt, ynt yer, Mawtzow? [*Marzo whimpers.*] Corse y'aw.

LADY CICELY [*to Sir Howard*]. Did you ever see such a helpless lot of poor creatures? [*She makes for the little door.*]

DRINKWATER. Eah! [*He runs to the door and places himself before it.*] Where mawt yr lidyship be gowin?

LADY CICELY. I'm going through every room in this castle to find a proper place to put that man. And now I'll tell you where you're going. You're going to get some water for Marzo, who is very thirsty. And then, when I've chosen a room for him, you're going to make a bed for him there.

DRINKWATER [*sarcastically*]. Ow! Henny ather little suvvice? Mike yrseolf at owm, y' knaow, lidy.

LADY CICELY [*considerately*]. Don't go if you'd rather not, Mr. Drinkwater. Perhaps you're too tired. [*Turning to the archway*] I'll ask Captain Brassbound: he won't mind.

DRINKWATER [*terrified, running after her and getting between her and the arch*]. Naow, naow! Naow, lidy: doesn't you goes disturbin the Kepn. Awll see to it.

LADY CICELY [*gravely*]. I was sure you would, Mr. Drinkwater. You have such a kind face. [*She turns back and goes out through the small door.*]

DRINKWATER [*looking after her*]. Garn!

SIR HOWARD [*to Drinkwater*]. Will you ask one of your friends to show me to my room whilst you are getting the water?

DRINKWATER [*insolently*]. Yr room! Ow: this ynt good enaf fr yr, ynt it? [*Ferociously*] Oo a you orderin abaht, ih?

SIR HOWARD [*rising quietly, and taking refuge between Redbrook and Johnson, whom he addresses*]. Can you find me a more private room than this?

JOHNSON [*shaking his head*]. I've no orders. You must wait til the capn comes, sir.

DRINKWATER [*following Sir Howard*]. Yuss; an whawl you're witin, yll tike your horders from me: see?

JOHNSON [*with slow severity, to Drinkwater*]. Look here: do you see three genlmen talkin to one another here, civil and private, eh?

DRINKWATER [*chapfallen*]. No offence, Miste Jornsn—

JOHNSON [*ominously*]. Ay; but there is offence. Where's your manners, you guttersnipe? [*Turning to Sir Howard*] That's the curse o this kind o life, sir: you got to associate with all sorts. My father, sir, was Capn Johnson o Hull—owned his own schooner, sir. We're mostly gentlemen here, sir, as you'll find, except the poor ignorant foreigner and that there scum of the submerged tenth. [*Contemptuously looking at Drinkwater*] he ain't nobody's son: he's only a offspring o coster folk or such.

DRINKWATER [*bursting into tears*]. Clawss feelin! thet's wot it is: clawss feelin! Wot are yer, arter all, bat a bloomin gang o west cowst cazhls (*casual ward paupers*)? [*Johnson is scandalized; and there is a general thrill of indignation.*] Better ev naow fembly, an rawse aht of it, lawk me, than ev a specble one and disgrice it, lawk you.

JOHNSON. Brandyfaced Jack: I name you for conduct and language unbecoming to a gentleman. Those who agree will signify the same in the usual manner.

ALL [*vehemently*]. Aye.

DRINKWATER [*wildly*]. Naow.

JOHNSON. Felix Drinkwater: are you goin out, or are you goin to wait til you're chucked out? You can cry in the passage. If you give any trouble, you'll have something to cry for.

[*They make a threatening movement towards Drinkwater.*]

DRINKWATER [*whimpering*]. You lee me alown: awm gowin. There's n'maw true demmecrettick feelin eah than there is in the owl bloomin M division of Noontn Corzwy coppers [*Newington Causeway policemen*].

[*As he slinks away in tears towards the arch, Brassbound enters. Drinkwater promptly shelters himself on the captain's left hand, the others retreating to the opposite side as Brassbound advances to the middle of the room. Sir Howard retires behind them and seats himself on the divan, much fatigued.*]

BRASSBOUND [*to Drinkwater*]. What are you snivelling at?

DRINKWATER. You awsk the wust cowst herristorcracy. They fawnds maw cornduck hanbecammin to a genlmn.

[*Brassbound is about to ask Johnson for an explanation, when Lady Cicely returns through the little door, and comes between Brassbound and Drinkwater.*]

LADY CICELY [*to Drinkwater*]. Have you fetched the water?

DRINKWATER. Yuss: nah you begin orn me. [*He weeps afresh.*]

LADY CICELY [*surprised*]. Oh! This won't do, Mr. Drinkwater. If you cry, I can't let you nurse your friend.

DRINKWATER [*frantic*]. Thet'll brike maw awt, wown't it nah? [*With a lamentable sob, he throws himself down on the divan, raging like an angry child.*]

LADY CICELY [*after contemplating him in astonishment for a moment*]. Captain Brassbound: are there any charwomen in the Atlas Mountains?

BRASSBOUND. There are people here who will work if you pay them, as there are elsewhere.

LADY CICELY. This castle is very romantic, Captain; but it hasn't had a spring cleaning since the Prophet lived in it. There's only one room I can put that wounded man into. It's the only one that has a bed in it: the second room on the right out of that passage.

BRASSBOUND [*haughtily*]. That is my room, madam.

LADY CICELY [*relieved*]. Oh, that's all right. It would have been so awkward if I had had to ask one of your men to turn out. You won't mind, I know. [*All the men stare at her. Even Drinkwater forgets his sorrows in his stupefaction.*]

BRASSBOUND. Pray, madam, have you made any arrangements for my accommodation?

LADY CICELY [*reassuringly*]. Yes: you can have my room instead wherever it may be: I'm sure you chose me a nice one. I must be near my patient; and I don't mind roughing it. Now I must have Marzo moved very carefully. Where is that truly gentlemanly Mr. Johnson?—oh, there you are, Mr. Johnson. [*She runs to Johnson, past Brassbound, who has to step back hastily out of her way with every expression frozen out of his face except one of extreme and indignant dumbfoundedness*]. Will you ask your strong friend to help you with Marzo: strong people are always so gentle.

JOHNSON. Let me introdooce Mr. Redbrook. Your ladyship may know his father, the very Rev. Dean Redbrook. [*He goes to Marzo.*]

REDBROOK. Happy to oblige you, Lady Cicely.

LADY CICELY [*shaking hands*]. Howdyedo? Of course I knew your father—Dunham, wasn't it? Were you ever called—

REDBROOK. The kid? Yes.

LADY CICELY. But why—

REDBROOK [*anticipating the rest of the question*]. Cards and drink, Lady Sis. [*He follows Johnson to the patient. Lady Cicely goes too.*] Now, Count Marzo. [*Marzo groans as Johnson and Redbrook raise him.*]

LADY CICELY. Now they're not hurting you, Marzo. They couldn't be more gentle.

MARZO. Drink.

LADY CICELY. I'll get you some water myself. Your friend Mr. Drinkwater was too overcome—take care of the corner—that's it— the second door on the right. [*She goes out with Marzo and his bearers through the little door.*]

BRASSBOUND [*still staring*]. Well, I a m damned—!

DRINKWATER [*getting up*]. Weoll, blimey!

BRASSBOUND [*turning irritably on him*]. What did you say?

DRINKWATER. Weoll, wot did yer sy yrseolf, kepn? Fust tawm aw yever see y' afride of ennybody. [*The others laugh.*]

BRASSBOUND. Afraid!

DRINKWATER [*maliciously*]. She's took y' bed from hander yr for a bloomin penny hawcemen. If y' ynt afride, let's eah yer speak ap to er wen she cams bawck agin.

BRASSBOUND [*to Sir Howard*]. I wish you to understand, Sir Howard, that in this castle, it is I who give orders, and no one else. Will you be good enough to let Lady Cicely Waynflete know that.

SIR HOWARD [*sitting up on the divan and pulling himself together*]. You will have ample opportunity for speaking to Lady Cicely yourself when she returns. [*Drinkwater chuckles: and the rest grin.*]

BRASSBOUND. My manners are rough, Sir Howard. I have no wish to frighten the lady.

SIR HOWARD. Captain Brassbound: if you can frighten Lady Cicely, you will confer a great obligation on her family. If she had any sense of danger, perhaps she would keep out of it.

BRASSBOUND. Well, sir, if she were ten Lady Cicelys, she must consult me while she is here.

DRINKWATER. Thet's rawt, kepn. Let's eah you steblish yr hawthority. [*Brassbound turns impatiently on him: He retreats remonstrating*] Nah, nah, nah!

SIR HOWARD. If you feel at all nervous, Captain Brassbound, I will mention the matter with pleasure.

BRASSBOUND. Nervous, sir! no. Nervousness is not in my line. You will find me perfectly capable of saying what I want to say—with considerable emphasis, if necessary. [*Sir Howard assents with a polite but incredulous nod.*]

DRINKWATER. Eah, eah!

[*Lady Cicely returns with Johnson and Redbrook. She carries a jar.*]

LADY CICELY [*stopping between the door and the arch*]. Now for the water. Where is it?

REDBROOK. There's a well in the courtyard. I'll come and work the bucket.

LADY CICELY. So good of you, Mr. Redbrook. [*She makes for the horseshoe arch, followed by Redbrook.*]

DRINKWATER. Nah, Kepn Brassbound: you got sathink to sy to the lidy, ynt yr?

LADY CICELY [*stopping*]. I'll come back to hear it presently, Captain. And oh, while I remember it [*coming forward between Brassbound and Drinkwater*], do please tell me Captain, if I interfere with your arrangements in any way. It I disturb you the least bit in the world, stop me at once. You have all the responsibility; and your comfort and your authority must be the first thing. You'll tell me, won't you?

BRASSBOUND [*awkwardly, quite beaten*]. Pray do as you please, madam.

LADY CICELY. Thank you. That's so like you, Captain. Thank you. Now, Mr. Redbrook! Show me the way to the well. [*She follows Redbrook out through the arch.*]

DRINKWATER. Yah! Yah! Shime! Beat baw a woman!

JOHNSON [*coming forward on Brassbound's right*]. What's wrong now?

DRINKWATER [*with an air of disappointment and disillusion*]. Down't awsk me, Miste Jornsn. The kepn's naow clawss arter all.

BRASSBOUND [*a little shamefacedly*]. What has she been fixing up in there, Johnson?

JOHNSON. Well: Marzo's in your bed. Lady wants to make a kitchen of the Sheikh's audience chamber, and to put me and the Kid handy in his bedroom in case Marzo gets erysipelas and breaks out violent. From what I can make out, she means to make herself matron of this institution. I spose it's all right, isn't it?

DRINKWATER. Yuss, an horder huz abaht as if we was keb tahts! An the kepn afride to talk bawck at er!

[*Lady Cicely returns with Redbrook. She carries the jar full of water.*]

LADY CICELY [*putting down the jar, and coming between Brassbound and Drinkwater as before*]. And now, Captain, before I go to poor Marzo, what have you to say to me?

BRASSBOUND. I! Nothing.

DRINKWATER. Down't fank it, gavner. Be a men!

LADY CICELY [*looking at Drinkwater, puzzled*]. Mr. Drinkwater said you had.

BRASSBOUND [*recovering himself*]. It was only this. That fellow there [*pointing to Drinkwater*] is subject to fits of insolence. If he is impertinent to your ladyship, or disobedient, you have my authority to order him as many kicks as you think good for him; and I will see that he gets them.

DRINKWATER [*lifting up his voice in protest*]. Nah, nah—

LADY CICELY. Oh, I couldn't think of such a thing, Captain Brassbound. I am sure it would hurt Mr. Drinkwater.

DRINKWATER [*lachrymosely*]. Lidy's hinkyp'ble o sich bawbrous usage.

LADY CICELY. But there's one thing I should like, if Mr. Drinkwater won't mind my mentioning it. It's so important if he's to attend on Marzo.

BRASSBOUND. What is that?

LADY CICELY. Well—you won't mind, Mr. Drinkwater, will you?

DRINKWATER [*suspiciously*]. Wot is it?

LADY CICELY. There would be so much less danger of erysipelas if you would be so good as to take a bath.

DRINKWATER [*aghast*]. A bawth!

BRASSBOUND [*in tones of command*]. Stand by, all hands. [*They stand by.*] Take that man and wash him. [*With a roar of laughter they seize him.*]

DRINKWATER [*in an agony of protest*]. Naow, naow. Look eah—

BRASSBOUND [*ruthlessly*]. In cold water.

DRINKWATER [*shrieking*]. Na-a-a-a-ow. Aw eawn't, aw toel yer. Naow. Aw sy, look eah. Naow, naow, naow, naow, naow, NAOW!!!

[*He is dragged away through the arch in a whirlwind of laughter, protests and tears.*]

LADY CICELY. I'm afraid he isn't used to it, poor fellow; but really it will do him good, Captain Brassbound. Now I must be off to my patient. [*She takes up her jar and goes out by the little door, leaving Brassbound and Sir Howard alone together.*]

SIR HOWARD [*rising*]. And now, Captain Brass—

BRASSBOUND [*cutting him short with a fierce contempt that astonishes him*]. I will attend to you presently. [*Calling*] Johnson. Send me Johnson there. And Osman. [*He pulls off his coat and throws it on the table, standing at his ease in his blue jersey.*]

SIR HOWARD [*after a momentary flush of anger, with a controlled force that compels Brassbound's attention in spite of himself*]. You seem to be in a strong position with reference to these men of yours.

BRASSBOUND. I am in a strong position with reference to everyone in this castle.

SIR HOWARD [*politely but threateningly*]. I have just been noticing that you think so. I do not agree with you. Her Majesty's Government, Captain Brassbound, has a strong arm and a long arm. If anything disagreeable happens to me or to my sister-in-law, that arm will be stretched out. If that happens you will not be in a strong position. Excuse my reminding you of it.

BRASSBOUND [*grimly*]. Much good may it do you! [*Johnson comes in through the arch.*] Where is Osman, the Sheikh's messenger? I want him too.

JOHNSON. Coming, Captain. He had a prayer to finish.

[*Osman, a tall, skinny, whiteclad, elderly Moor, appears in the archway.*]

BRASSBOUND. Osman Ali [*Osman comes forward between Brassbound and Johnson*]: you have seen this unbeliever [*indicating Sir Howard*] come in with us?

OSMAN. Yea, and the shameless one with the naked face, who flattered my countenance and offered me her hand.

JOHNSON. Yes; and you took it too, Johnny, didn't you?

BRASSBOUND. Take horse, then; and ride fast to your master the Sheikh Sidi el Assif.—

OSMAN [*proudly*]. Kinsman to the Prophet.

BRASSBOUND. Tell him what you have seen here. That is all. Johnson: give him a dollar; and note the hour of his going, that his master may know how fast he rides.

OSMAN. The believer's word shall prevail with Allah and his servant Sidi el Assif.

BRASSBOUND. Off with you.

OSMAN. Make good thy master's word ere I go out from his presence, O Johnson el Hull.

JOHNSON. He wants the dollar.

[*Brassbound gives Osman a coin.*]

OSMAN [*bowing*]. Allah will make hell easy for the friend of Sidi el Assif and his servant. [*He goes out through the arch.*]

BRASSBOUND [*to Johnson*]. Keep the men out of this until the Sheikh comes. I have business to talk over. When he does come, we must keep together all: Sidi el Assif's natural instinct will be to cut every Christian throat here.

JOHNSON. We look to you, Captain, to square him, since you invited him over.

BRASSBOUND. You can depend on me; and you know it, I think.

JOHNSON [*phlegmatically*]. Yes: we know it. [*He is going out when Sir Howard speaks.*]

SIR HOWARD. You know also, Mr. Johnson, I hope, that you can depend on m e.

JOHNSON [*turning*]. On you, sir?

SIR HOWARD. Yes: on me. If my throat is cut, the Sultan of Morocco may send Sidi's head with a hundred thousand dollars blood-money to the Colonial Office; but it will not be enough to save his kingdom—any more than it would saw your life, if your Captain here did the same thing.

JOHNSON [*struck*]. Is that so, Captain?

BRASSBOUND. I know the gentleman's value—better perhaps than he knows it himself. I shall not lose sight of it.

[*Johnson nods gravely, and is going out when Lady Cicely returns softly by the little door and calls to him in a whisper. She has taken off her travelling things and put on an apron. At her chatelaine is a case of sewing materials.*]

LADY CICELY. Mr. Johnson. [*He turns.*] I've got Marzo to sleep. Would you mind asking the gentlemen not to make a noise under his window in the courtyard.

JOHNSON. Right, maam. [*He goes out.*]

[*Lady Cicely sits down at the tiny table, and begins stitching at a sling bandage for Marzo's arm. Brassbound walks up and down on her right, muttering to himself so ominously that Sir Howard quietly gets out of his way by crossing to the other side and sitting down on the second saddle seat.*]

SIR HOWARD. Are you yet able to attend to me for a moment, Captain Brassbound?

BRASSBOUND [*still walking about*]. What do you want?

SIR HOWARD. Well, I am afraid I want a little privacy, and, if you will allow me to say so, a little civility. I am greatly obliged to you for bringing us safely off to-day when we were attacked. So far, you have carried out your contract. But since we have been your guests here, your tone and that of the worst of your men has changed—intentionally changed, I think.

BRASSBOUND [*stopping abruptly and flinging the announcement at him*]. You are not my guest: you are my prisoner.

SIR HOWARD. Prisoner!

[*Lady Cicely, after a single glance up, continues stitching, apparently quite unconcerned.*]

BRASSBOUND. I warned you. You should have taken my warning.

SIR HOWARD [*immediately taking the tone of cold disgust for moral delinquency*]. Am I to understand, then, that you are a brigand? Is this a matter of ransom?

BRASSBOUND [*with unaccountable intensity*]. All the wealth of England shall not ransom you.

SIR HOWARD. Then what do you expect to gain by this?

BRASSBOUND. Justice on a thief and a murderer.

[*Lady Cicely lays down her work and looks up anxiously.*]

SIR HOWARD [*deeply outraged, rising with venerable dignity*]. Sir: do you apply those terms to me?

BRASSBOUND. I do. [*He turns to Lady Cicely, and adds, pointing contemptuously to Sir Howard*] Look at him. You would not take this virtuously indignant gentleman for the uncle of a brigand, would you?

[*Sir Howard starts. The shock is too much for him: he sits down again, looking very old; and his hands tremble; but his eyes and mouth are intrepid, resolute, and angry.*]

LADY CICELY. Uncle! What do you mean?

BRASSBOUND. Has he never told you about my mother? this fellow who puts on ermine and scarlet and calls himself Justice.

SIR HOWARD [*almost voiceless*]. You are the son of that woman!

BRASSBOUND [*fiercely*]. "That woman!" [*He makes a movement as if to rush at Sir Howard.*]

LADY CICELY [*rising quickly and putting her hand on his arm*]. Take care. You mustn't strike an old man.

BRASSBOUND [*raging*]. He did not spare my mother—"that woman," he calls her—because of her sex. I will not spare him because of his age. [*Lowering his tone to one of sullen vindictiveness*] But I am not going to strike him. [*Lady Cicely releases him, and sits down, much perplexed. Brassbound continues, with an evil glance at Sir Howard*] I shall do no more than justice.

SIR HOWARD [*recovering his voice and vigor*]. Justice! I think you mean vengeance, disguised as justice by your passions.

BRASSBOUND. To many and many a poor wretch in the dock you have brought vengeance in that disguise—the vengeance of society, disguised as justice by its passions. Now the justice you have outraged meets you disguised as vengeance. How do you like it?

SIR HOWARD. I shall meet it, I trust, as becomes an innocent man and an upright judge. What do you charge against me?

BRASSBOUND. I charge you with the death of my mother and the theft of my inheritance.

SIR HOWARD. As to your inheritance, sir, it was yours whenever you came forward to claim it. Three minutes ago I did not know of your existence. I affirm that most solemnly. I never knew—never dreamt—that my brother Miles left a son. As to your mother, her case was a hard one—perhaps the hardest that has come within even my experience. I mentioned it, as such, to Mr. Rankin, the missionary, the evening we met you. As to her death, you know—you must know—that she died in her native country, years after our last meeting. Perhaps you were too young to know that she could hardly have expected to live long.

BRASSBOUND. You mean that she drank.

SIR HOWARD. *I* did not say so. I do not think she was always accountable for what she did.

BRASSBOUND. Yes: she was mad too; and whether drink drove her to madness or madness drove her to drink matters little. The question is, who drove her to both?

SIR HOWARD. I presume the dishonest agent who seized her estate did. I repeat, it was a hard case—a frightful injustice. But it could not be remedied.

BRASSBOUND. You told her so. When she would not take that false answer you drove her from your doors. When she exposed you in the street and threatened to take with her own hands the redress the law denied her, you had her imprisoned, and forced her to write you an apology and leave the country to regain her liberty and save herself from a lunatic asylum. And when she was gone, and dead, and forgotten, you found for yourself the remedy you could not find for her. You recovered the estate easily enough then, robber and rascal that you are. Did he tell the missionary that, Lady Cicely, eh?

LADY CICELY [*sympathetically*]. Poor woman! [*To Sir Howard*] Couldn't you have helped her, Howard?

SIR HOWARD. No. This man may be ignorant enough to suppose that when I was a struggling barrister I could do everything I did when I was Attorney General. You know better. There is some excuse for his mother. She was an uneducated Brazilian, knowing nothing of English society, and driven mad by injustice.

BRASSBOUND. Your defence—

SIR HOWARD [*interrupting him determinedly*]. I do not defend myself. I call on you to obey the law.

BRASSBOUND. I intend to do so. The law of the Atlas Mountains is administered by the Sheikh Sidi el Assif. He will be here within an hour. He is a judge like yourself. You can talk law to him. He will give you both the law and the prophets.

SIR HOWARD. Does he know what the power of England is?

BRASSBOUND. He knows that the Mahdi killed my master Gordon, and that the Mahdi died in his bed and went to paradise.

SIR HOWARD. Then he knows also that England's vengeance was on the Mahdi's track.

BRASSBOUND. Ay, on the track of the railway from the Cape to Cairo. Who are you, that a nation should go to war for you? If you are missing, what will your newspapers say? A foolhardy tourist. What will your learned friends at the bar say? That it was time for you to make room for younger and better men. You a national hero! You had better find a goldfield in the Atlas Mountains. Then all the governments of Europe will rush to your rescue. Until then, take care of yourself; for you are going to see at last the hypocrisy in the sanctimonious speech of the judge who is sentencing you, instead of the despair in the white face of the wretch you are recommending to the mercy of your God.

SIR HOWARD [*deeply and personally offended by this slight to his profession, and for the first time throwing away his assumed dignity and rising to approach Brassbound with his fists clenched; so that Lady Cicely lifts one eye from her work to assure herself that the table is between them*]. I have no more to say to you, sir. I am not afraid of you, nor of any bandit with whom you may be in league. As to your property, it is ready for you as soon as you come to your senses and claim it as your father's heir. Commit a crime, and you will become an outlaw, and not only lose the property, but shut the doors of civilization against yourself for ever.

BRASSBOUND. I will not sell my mother's revenge for ten properties.

LADY CICELY [*placidly*]. Besides, really, Howard, as the property now costs £150 a year to keep up instead of bringing in anything, I am afraid it would not be of much use to him. [*Brassbound stands amazed at this revelation.*]

SIR HOWARD [*taken aback*]. I must say, Cicely, I think you might have chosen a more suitable moment to mention that fact.

BRASSBOUND [*with disgust*]. Agh! Trickster! Lawyer! Even the price you offer for your life is to be paid in false coin. [Calling] Hallo there! Johnson! Redbrook! Some of you there! [*To Sir Howard*] You ask for a little privacy: you shall have it. I will not endure the company of such a fellow—

SIR HOWARD [*very angry, and full of the crustiest pluck*]. You insult me, sir. You are a rascal. You are a rascal.

[*Johnson, Redbrook, and a few others come in through the arch.*]

BRASSBOUND. Take this man away.

JOHNSON. Where are we to put him?

BRASSBOUND. Put him where you please so long as you can find him when he is wanted.

SIR HOWARD. You will be laid by the heels yet, my friend.

REDBROOK [*with cheerful tact*]. Tut tut, Sir Howard: what's the use of talking back? Come along: we'll make you comfortable.

[*Sir Howard goes out through the arch between Johnson and Redbrook, muttering wrathfully. The rest, except Brassbound and Lady Cicely, follow.*

Brassbound walks up and down the room, nursing his indignation. In doing so he unconsciously enters upon an unequal contest with Lady Cicely, who sits quietly stitching. It soon becomes clear that a tranquil woman can go on sewing longer than an angry man can go on fuming. Further, it begins to dawn on Brassbound's wrath-blurred perception that Lady Cicely has at some unnoticed stage in the proceedings finished Marzo's bandage, and is now stitching a coat. He stops; glances at his shirtsleeves; finally realizes the situation.]

BRASSBOUND. What are you doing there, madam?

LADY CICELY. Mending your coat, Captain Brassbound.

BRASSBOUND. I have no recollection of asking you to take that trouble.

LADY CICELY. No: I don't suppose you even knew it was torn. Some men are born untidy. You cannot very well receive Sidi el—what's his name?—with your sleeve half out.

BRASSBOUND [*disconcerted*]. I—I don't know how it got torn.

LADY CICELY. You should not get virtuously indignant with people. It bursts clothes more than anything else, Mr. Hallam.

BRASSBOUND [*flushing, quickly*]. I beg you will not call me Mr. Hallam. I hate the name.

LADY CICELY. Black Paquito is your pet name, isn't it?

BRASSBOUND [*huffily*]. I am not usually called so to my face.

LADY CICELY [*turning the coat a little*]. I'm so sorry. [*She takes another piece of thread and puts it into her needle, looking placidly and reflectively upward meanwhile.*] Do you know, You are wonderfully like your uncle.

BRASSBOUND. Damnation!

LADY CICELY. Eh?

BRASSBOUND. If I thought my veins contained a drop of his black blood, I would drain them empty with my knife. I have no relations. I had a mother: that was all.

LADY CICELY [*unconvinced*] I daresay you have your mother's complexion. But didn't you notice Sir Howard's temper, his doggedness, his high spirit: above all, his belief in ruling people by force, as you rule your men; and in revenge and punishment, just as you want to revenge your mother? Didn't you recognize yourself in that?

BRASSBOUND [*startled*]. Myself!—in that!

LADY CECILY [*returning to the tailoring question as if her last remark were of no consequence whatever*]. Did this sleeve catch you at all under the arm? Perhaps I had better make it a little easier for you.

BRASSBOUND [*irritably*]. Let my coat alone. It will do very well as it is. Put it down.

LADY CICILY. Oh, don't ask me to sit doing nothing. It bores me so.

BRASSBOUND. In Heaven's name then, do what you like! Only don't worry me with it.

LADY CICELY. I'm so sorry. All the Hallams are irritable.

BRASSBOUND [*penning up his fury with difficulty*]. As I have already said, that remark has no application to me.

LADY CICELY [*resuming her stitching*]. That's so funny! They all hate to be told that they are like one another.

BRASSBOUND [*with the beginnings of despair in his voice*]. Why did you come here? My trap was laid for him, not for you. Do you know the danger you are in?

LADY CICELY. There's always a danger of something or other. Do you think it's worth bothering about?

BRASSBOUND [*scolding her*]. Do I think! Do you think my coat's worth mending?

LADY CICELY [*prosaically*]. Oh yes: it's not so far gone as that.

BRASSBOUND. Have you any feeling? Or are you a fool?

LADY CICELY. I'm afraid I'm a dreadful fool. But I can't help it. I was made so, I suppose.

BRASSBOUND. Perhaps you don't realize that your friend my good uncle will be pretty fortunate if he is allowed to live out his life as a slave with a set of chains on him?

LADY CICELY. Oh, I don't know about that, Mr. H—I mean Captain Brassbound. Men are always thinking that they are going to do something grandly wicked to their enemies; but when it comes to the point, really bad men are just as rare as really good ones.

BRASSBOUND. You forget that I am like my uncle, according to you. Have you any doubt as to the reality of HIS badness?

LADY CICELY. Bless me! your uncle Howard is one of the most harmless of men—much nicer than most professional people. Of course he does dreadful things as a judge; but then if you take a man and pay him £5,000 a year to be wicked, and praise him for it, and have policemen and courts and laws and juries to drive him into it so that he can't help doing it, what can you expect? Sir

Howard's all right when he's left to himself. We caught a burglar one night at Waynflete when he was staying with us; and I insisted on his locking the poor man up until the police came, in a room with a window opening on the lawn. The man came back next day and said he must return to a life of crime unless I gave him a job in the garden; and I did. It was much more sensible than giving him ten years penal servitude: Howard admitted it. So you see he's not a bit bad really.

BRASSBOUND. He had a fellow feeling for a thief, knowing he was a thief himself. Do you forget that he sent my mother to prison?

LADY CICELY [*softly*]. Were you very fond of your poor mother, and always very good to her?

BRASSBOUND [*rather taken aback*]. I was not worse than other sons, I suppose.

LADY CICELY [*opening her eyes very widely*]. Oh! Was that all?

BRASSBOUND [*exculpating himself, full of gloomy remembrances*]. You don't understand. It was not always possible to be very tender with my mother. She had unfortunately a very violent temper; and she—she—

LADY CICELY. Yes: so you told Howard. [*With genuine pity for him*] You must have had a very unhappy childhood.

BRASSBOUND [*grimily*]. Hell. That was what my childhood was. Hell.

LADY CICELY. Do you think she would really have killed Howard, as she threatened, if he hadn't sent her to prison?

BRASSBOUND [*breaking out again, with a growing sense of being morally trapped*]. What if she did? Why did he rob her? Why did he not help her to get the estate, as he got it for himself afterwards?

LADY CICELY. He says he couldn't, you know. But perhaps the real reason was that he didn't like her. You know, don't you, that if you don't like people you think of all the reasons for not helping them, and if you like them you think of all the opposite reasons.

BRASSBOUND. But his duty as a brother!

LADY CICELY. Are you going to do your duty as a nephew?

BRASSBOUND. Don't quibble with me. I am going to do my duty as a son; and you know it.

LADY CICELY. But I should have thought that the time for that was in your mother's lifetime, when you could have been kind and forbearing with her. Hurting your uncle won't do her any good, you know.

BRASSBOUND. It will teach other scoundrels to respect widows and orphans. Do you forget that there is such a thing as justice?

LADY CICELY [*gaily shaking out the finished coat*]. Oh, if you are going to dress yourself in ermine and call yourself Justice, I give you up. You are just your uncle over again; only he gets £5,000 a year for it, and you do it for nothing. [*She holds the coat up to see whether any further repairs are needed.*]

BRASSBOUND [*sulkily*]. You twist my words very cleverly. But no man or woman has ever changed me.

LADY CICELY. Dear me! That must be very nice for the people you deal with, because they can always depend on you; but isn't it rather inconvenient for yourself when you change your mind?

BRASSBOUND. I never change my mind.

LADY CICELY [*rising with the coat in her hands*]. Oh! Oh!! Nothing will ever persuade me that you are as pigheaded as that.

BRASSBOUND [*offended*]. Pigheaded!

LADY CICELY [*with quick, caressing apology*]. No, no, no. I didn't mean that. Firm! Unalterable! Resolute! Iron-willed! Stonewall Jackson! That's the idea, isn't it?

BRASSBOUND [*hopelessly*]. You are laughing at me.

LADY CICELY. No: trembling, I assure you. Now will you try this on for me: I'm so afraid I have made it too tight under the arm. [*She holds it behind him.*]

BRASSBOUND [*obeying mechanically*]. You take me for a fool I think. [*He misses the sleeve.*]

LADY CICELY. No: all men look foolish when they are feeling for their sleeves.

BRASSBOUND. Agh! [*He turns and snatches the coat from her; then puts it on himself and buttons the lowest button.*]

LADY CICELY [*horrified*]. Stop. No. You must NEVER pull a coat at the skirts, Captain Brassbound: it spoils the sit of it. Allow me. [*She pulls the lapels of his coat vigorously forward*] Put back your shoulders. [*He frowns, but obeys.*] That's better. [*She buttons the top button.*] Now button the rest from the top down. Does it catch you at all under the arm?

BRASSBOUND [*miserably—all resistance beaten out of him*]. No.

LADY CICELY. That's right. Now before I go back to poor Marzo, say thank you to me for mending your jacket, like a nice polite sailor.

BRASSBOUND [*sitting down at the table in great agitation*]. Damn you! you have belittled my whole life to me. [*He bows his head on his hands, convulsed.*]

LADY CICELY [*quite understanding, and putting her hand kindly on his shoulder*]. Oh no. I am sure you have done lots of kind things and brave things, if you could only recollect them. With Gordon for instance? Nobody can belittle that.

[*He looks up at her for a moment; then kisses her hand. She presses his and turns away with her eyes so wet that she sees Drinkwater, coming in through the arch just then, with a prismatic halo round him. Even when she sees him clearly, she hardly recognizes him; for he is ludicrously clean and smoothly brushed; and his hair, formerly mud color, is now a lively red.*]

DRINKWATER. Look eah, kepn. [*Brassbound springs up and recovers himself quickly.*] Eahs the bloomin Shike jest appeahd on the orawzn wiv abaht fifty men. Thy'll be eah insawd o ten minnits, they will.

LADY CICELY. The Sheikh!

BRASSBOUND. Sidi el Assif and fifty men! [*To Lady Cicely*] You were too late: I gave you up my vengeance when it was no longer in my hand. [*To Drinkwater*] Call all hands to stand by and shut the gates. Then all here to me for orders; and bring the prisoner.

DRINKWATER. Rawt, kepn. [*He runs out.*]

LADY CICELY. Is there really any danger for Howard?

BRASSBOUND. Yes. Danger for all of us unless I keep to my bargain with this fanatic.

LADY CICELY. What bargain?

BRASSBOUND. I pay him so much a head for every party I escort through to the interior. In return he protects me and lets my caravans alone. But I have sworn an oath to him to take only Jews and true believers—no Christians, you understand.

LADY CICELY. Then why did you take us?

BRASSBOUND. I took my uncle on purpose—and sent word to Sidi that he was here.

LADY CICELY. Well, that's a pretty kettle of fish, isn't it?

BRASSBOUND. I will do what I can to save him—and you. But I fear my repentance has come too late, as repentance usually does.

LADY CICELY [*cheerfully*]. Well, I must go and look after Marzo, at all events. [*She goes out through the little door. Johnson, Redbrook and the rest come in through the arch, with Sir Howard, still very crusty and determined. He keeps close to Johnson, who comes to Brassbound's right, Redbrook taking the other side.*]

BRASSBOUND. Where's Drinkwater?

JOHNSON. On the lookout. Look here, Capn: we don't half like this job. The gentleman has been talking to us a bit; and we think that he i s a gentleman, and talks straight sense.

REDBROOK. Righto, Brother Johnson. [*To Brassbound*] Won't do, governor. Not good enough.

BRASSBOUND [*fiercely*]. Mutiny, eh?

REDBROOK. Not at all, governor. Don't talk Tommy rot with Brother Sidi only five minutes gallop off. Can't hand over an Englishman to a nigger to have his throat cut.

BRASSBOUND [*unexpectedly acquiescing*]. Very good. You know, I suppose, that if you break my bargain with Sidi, you'll have to defend this place and fight for your lives in five minutes. That can't be done without discipline: you know that too. I'll take my part with the rest under whatever leader you are willing to obey. So choose your captain and look sharp about it. [*Murmurs of surprise and discontent.*]

VOICES. No, no. Brassbound must command.

BRASSBOUND. You're wasting your five minutes. Try Johnson.

JOHNSON. No. I haven't the head for it.

BRASSBOUND. Well, Redbrook.

REDBROOK. Not this Johnny, thank you. Haven't character enough.

BRASSBOUND. Well, there's Sir Howard Hallam for You! He has character enough.

A VOICE. He's too old.

ALL. No, no. Brassbound, Brassbound.

JOHNSON. There's nobody but you, Captain.

REDRROOK. The mutiny's over, governor. You win, hands down.

BRASSBOUND [*turning on them*]. Now listen, you, all of you. If I am to command here, I am going to do what I like, not what you like. I'll give this gentleman here to Sidi or to the devil if I choose. I'll not be intimidated or talked back to. Is that understood?

REDBROOK [*diplomatically*]. He's offered a present of five hundred quid if he gets safe back to Mogador, governor. Excuse my mentioning it.

SIR HOWARD. Myself and Lady Cicely.

BRASSBOUND. What! A judge compound a felony! You greenhorns, he is more likely to send you all to penal servitude if you are fools enough to give him the chance.

VOICES. So he would. Whew! [*Murmurs of conviction.*]

REDBROOK. Righto, governor. That's the ace of trumps.

BRASSBOUND [*to Sir Howard*]. Now, have you any other card to play? Any other bribe? Any other threat? Quick. Time presses.

SIR HOWARD. My life is in the hands of Providence. Do your worst.

BRASSBOUND. Or my best. I still have that choice.

DRINKWATER [*running in*]. Look eah, kepn. Eah's anather lot cammin from the sahth heast. Hunnerds of em, this tawm. The owl dezzit is lawk a bloomin Awd Pawk demonstration. Aw blieve it's the Kidy from Kintorfy. [*General alarm. All look to Brassbound.*]

BRASSBOUND [*eagerly*]. The Cadi! How far off?

DRINKWATER. Matter o two mawl.

BRASSBOUND. We're saved. Open the gates to the Sheikh.

DRINKWATER [*appalled, almost in tears*]. Naow, naow. Lissen, kepn [*Pointing to Sir Howard*]: e'll give huz fawv unnerd red uns. [*To the others*] Ynt yer spowk to im, Miste Jornsn—Miste Redbrook—

BRASSBOUND [*cutting him short*]. Now then, do you understand plain English? Johnson and Redbrook: take what men you want and open the gates to the Sheikh. Let him come straight to me. Look alive, will you.

JOHNSON. Ay ay, sir.

REDBROOK. Righto, governor.

[*They hurry out, with a few others. Drinkwater stares after them, dumbfounded by their obedience.*]

BRASSBOUND [*taking out a pistol*]. You wanted to sell me to my prisoner, did you, you dog.

DRINKWATER [*falling on his knees with a yell*]. Naow! [*Brassbound turns on him as if to kick him. He scrambles away and takes refuge behind Sir Howard.*]

BRASSBOUND. Sir Howard Hallam: you have one chance left. The Cadi of Kintafi stands superior to the Sheikh as the responsible governor of the whole province. It is the Cadi who will be sacrificed by the Sultan if England demands satisfaction for any injury to you. If we can hold the Sheikh in parley until the Cadi arrives, you may frighten the Cadi into forcing the Sheikh to release you. The Cadi's coming is a lucky chance for you.

SIR HOWARD. If it were a real chance, you would not tell me of it. Don't try to play cat and mouse with me, man.

DRINKWATER [*aside to Sir Howard, as Brassbound turns contemptuously away to the other side of the room*]. It ynt mach of a chawnst, Sr Ahrd. But if there was a ganbowt in Mogador Awbr, awd put a bit on it, aw would.

[*Johnson, Redbrook, and the others return, rather mistrustfully ushering in Sidi el Assif, attended by Osman and a troop of Arabs. Brassbound's men keep together on the archway side, backing their captain. Sidi's followers cross the room behind the table and assemble near Sir Howard, who stands his ground. Drinkwater runs across to Brassbound and stands at his elbow as he turns to face Sidi.*

Sidi el Aasif, clad in spotless white, is a nobly handsome Arab, hardly thirty, with fine eyes, bronzed complexion, and instinctively dignified carriage. He places himself between the two groups, with Osman in attendance at his right hand.]

OSMAN [*pointing out Sir Howard*]. This is the infidel Cadi. [*Sir Howard bows to Sidi, but, being an infidel, receives only the haughtiest stare in acknowledgement.*] This [*pointing to Brassbound*] is Brassbound the Franguestani captain, the servant of Sidi.

DRINKWATER [*not to be outdone, points out the Sheikh and Osman to Brassbound*]. This eah is the Commawnder of the Fythful an is Vizzeer Hosman.

SIDI. Where is the woman?

OSMAN. The shameless one is not here.

BRASSBOUND. Sidi el Assif, kinsman of the Prophet: you are welcome.

REDBROOK [*with much aplomb*]. There is no majesty and no might save in Allah, the Glorious, the Great!

DRINKWATER. Eah, eah!

OSMAN [*to Sidi*]. The servant of the captain makes his profession of faith as a true believer.

SIDI. It is well.

BRASSBOUND [*aside to Redbrook*]. Where did you pick that up?

REDRROOK [*aside to Brassbound*]. Captain Burton's Arabian Nights—copy in the library of the National Liberal Club.

LADY CICELY [*calling without*]. Mr. Drinkwater. Come and help me with Marzo. [*The Sheikh pricks up his ears. His nostrils and eyes expand.*]

OSMAN. The shameless one!

BRASSBOUND [*to Drinkwater, seizing him by the collar and slinging him towards the door*]. Off with you.

[*Drinkwater goes out through the little door.*]

OSMAN. Shall we hide her face before she enters?
SIDI. NO.

[*Lady Cicely, who has resumed her travelling equipment, and has her hat slung across her arm, comes through the little door supporting Marzo, who is very white, but able to get about. Drinkwater has his other arm. Redbrook hastens to relieve Lady Cicely of Marzo, taking him into the group behind Brassbound. Lady Cicely comes forward between Brassbound and the Sheikh, to whom she turns affably.*]

LADY CICELY [*proffering her hand*]. Sidi el Assif, isn't it? How dye do? [*He recoils, blushing somewhat.*]
OSMAN [*scandalized*]. Woman; touch not the kinsman of the Prophet.
LADY CICELY. Oh, I see. I'm being presented at court. Very good. [*She makes a presentation curtsey.*]
REDBROOK. Sidi el Assif: this is one of the mighty women Sheikhs of Franguestan. She goes unveiled among Kings; and only princes may touch her hand.
LADY CICELY. Allah upon thee, Sidi el Assif! Be a good little Sheikh, and shake hands.
SIDI [*timidly touching her hand*]. Now this is a wonderful thing, and worthy to be chronicled with the story of Solomon and the Queen of Sheba. Is it not so, Osman Ali?
OSMAN. Allah upon thee, master! it is so.
SIDI. Brassbound Ali: the oath of a just man fulfils itself without many words. The infidel Cadi, thy captive, falls to my share.
BRASSBOUND [*firmly*]. It cannot be, Sidi el Assif. [*Sidi's brows contract gravely.*] The price of his blood will be required of our lord the Sultan. I will take him to Morocco and deliver him up there.
SIDI [*impressively*]. Brassbound: I am in mine own house and amid mine own people. I am the Sultan here. Consider what you say; for when my word goes forth for life or death, it may not be recalled.
BRASSBOUND. Sidi el Assif: I will buy the man from you at what price you choose to name; and if I do not pay faithfully, you shall take my head for his.

SIDI. It is well. You shall keep the man, and give me the woman in payment.

SIR HOWARD AND BRASSBOUND [*with the same impulse*]. No, no.

LADY CICELY [*eagerly*]. Yes, yes. Certainly, Mr. Sidi. Certainly.

[*Sidi smiles gravely.*]

SIR HOWARD. Impossible.

BRASSBOUND. You don't know what you're doing.

LADY CICELY. Oh, don't I? I've not crossed Africa and stayed with six cannibal chiefs for nothing. [*To the Sheikh*] It's all right, Mr. Sidi: I shall be delighted.

SIR HOWARD. You are mad. Do you suppose this man will treat you as a European gentleman would?

LADY CICELY. No: he'll treat me like one of Nature's gentlemen: look at his perfectly splendid face! [*Addressing Osman as if he were her oldest and most attached retainer.*] Osman: be sure you choose me a good horse; and get a nice strong camel for my luggage.

[*Osman, after a moment of stupefaction, hurries out. Lady Cicely puts on her hat and pins it to her hair, the Sheikh gazing at her during the process with timid admiration.*]

DRINKWATER [*chuckling*]. She'll mawch em all to church next Sunder lawk a bloomin lot o' cherrity kids: you see if she doesn't.

LADY CICELY [*busily*]. Goodbye, Howard: don't be anxious about me; and above all, don't bring a parcel of men with guns to rescue me. I shall be all right now that I am getting away from the escort. Captain Brassbound: I rely on you to see that Sir Howard gets safe to Mogador. [*Whispering*] Take your hand off that pistol. [*He takes his hand out of his pocket, reluctantly.*] Goodbye.

[*A tumult without. They all turn apprehensively to the arch. Osman rushes in.*]

OSMAN. The Cadi, the Cadi. He is in anger. His men are upon us. Defend—

[*The Cadi, a vigorous, fatfeatured, choleric, whitehaired and bearded elder, rushes in, cudgel in hand, with an overwhelming retinue, and silences Osman with a sounding thwack. In a moment the back of the room is crowded with his followers. The Sheikh retreats a little towards his men; and the Cadi comes impetuously forward between him and Lady Cicely.*]

THE CADI. Now woe upon thee, Sidi el Assif, thou child of mischief!

SIDI [*sternly*]. Am I a dog, Muley Othman, that thou speakest thus to me?

THE CADI. Wilt thou destroy thy country, and give us all into the hands of them that set the sea on fire but yesterday with their ships of war? Where are the Franguestani captives?

LADY CICELY. Here we are, Cadi. How dye do?

THE CADI. Allah upon thee, thou moon at the full! Where is thy kinsman, the Cadi of Franguestan? I am his friend, his servant. I come on behalf of my master the Sultan to do him honor, and to cast down his enemies.

SIR HOWARD. You are very good, I am sure.

SIDI [*graver than ever*]. Muley Othman—

TAE CADI [*fumbling in his breast*]. Peace, peace, thou inconsiderate one. [*He takes out a letter.*]

BRASSBOUND. Cadi—

THE CADI. Oh thou dog, thou, thou accursed Brassbound, son of a wanton: it is thou hast led Sidi el Assif into this wrongdoing. Read this writing that thou hast brought upon me from the commander of the warship.

BRASSBOUND. Warship! [*He takes the letter and opens it, his men whispering to one another very low-spiritedly meanwhile.*]

REDBROOK. Warship! Whew!

JOHNSON. Gunboat, praps.

DRINKWATER. Lawk bloomin Worterleoo buses, they are, on this cowst.

[*Brassbound folds up the letter, looking glum.*]

SIR HOWARD [*sharply*]. Well, sir, are we not to have the benefit of that letter? Your men are waiting to hear it, I think.

BRASSBOUND. It is not a British ship. [*Sir Howard's face falls.*]

LADY CICELY. What is it, then?

BRASSBOUND. An American cruiser. The Santiago.

THE CADI [*tearing his beard*]. Woe! alas! it is where they set the sea on fire.

SIDI. Peace, Muley Othman: Allah is still above us.

JOHNSON. Would you mind readin it to us, capn?

BRASSBOUND [*grimly*]. Oh, I'll read it to you. "Mogador Harbor. 26 Sept. 1899. Captain Hamlin Kearney, of the cruiser Santiago, presents the compliments of the United States to the Cadi Muley Othman el Kintafi, and announces that he is coming to look for the two British travellers Sir Howard Hallam and Lady Cicely Waynflete, in the Cadi's jurisdiction. As the search will be conducted with machine guns, the prompt return of the travellers to Mogador Harbor will save much trouble to all parties."

THE CADI. As I live, O Cadi, and thou, moon of loveliness, ye shall be led back to Mogador with honor. And thou, accursed Brassbound, shall go thither a prisoner in chains, thou and thy people. [*Brassbound and his men make a movement to defend themselves.*] Seize them.

LADY CICELY. Oh, please don't fight. [*Brassbound, seeing that his men are hopelessly outnumbered, makes no resistance. They are made prisoners by the Cadi's followers.*]

SIDI [*attempting to draw his scimitar*]. The woman is mine: I will not forego her. [*He is seized and overpowered after a Homeric struggle.*]

SIR HOWARD [*drily*]. I told you you were not in a strong position, Captain Brassbound. [*Looking implacably at him.*] You are laid by the heels, my friend, as I said you would be.

LADY CICELY. But I assure you—

BRASSBOUND [*interrupting her*]. What have you to assure him of? You persuaded me to spare him. Look at his face. Will you be able to persuade him to spare me?

ACT III

*Torrid forenoon filtered through small Moorish windows high up
in the adobe walls of the largest room in Leslie Rankin's house. A clean
cool room, with the table [a Christian article] set in the middle, a
presidentially elbowed chair behind it, and an inkstand and paper
ready for the sitter. A couple of cheap American chairs right and left of
the table, facing the same way as the presidential chair, give a judicial
aspect to the arrangement. Rankin is placing a little tray with a jug and
some glasses near the inkstand when Lady Cicely's voice is heard at the
door, which is behind him in the corner to his right.*

LADE CICELY. Good morning. May I come in?

RANKIN. Certainly. [*She comes in, to the nearest end of the table. She
has discarded all travelling equipment, and is dressed exactly as
she might be in Surrey on a very hot day.*] Sit ye doon, Leddy
Ceecily.

LADY CICELY [*sitting down*]. How nice you've made the room for
the inquiry!

RANKIN [*doubtfully*]. I could wish there were more chairs. Yon
American captain will preside in this; and that leaves but one for
Sir Howrrd and one for your leddyship. I could almost be tempted
to call it a maircy that your friend that owns the yacht has sprained
his ankle and cannot come. I misdoubt me it will not look judeecial
to have Captain Kearney's officers squatting on the floor.

LADY CICELY. Oh, they won't mind. What about the prisoners?

RANKIN. They are to be broat here from the town gaol presently.

LADY CICELY. And where is that silly old Cadi, and my handsome
Sheikh Sidi? I must see them before the inquiry, or they'll give
Captain Kearney quite a false impression of what happened.

RANKIN. But ye cannot see them. They decamped last night, back to
their castles in the Atlas.

LADY CICELY [*delighted*]. No!

RANKIN. Indeed and they did. The poor Cadi is so terrified by all he
has haird of the destruction of the Spanish fleet, that he daren't
trust himself in the captain's hands. [*Looking reproachfully at her*]
On your journey back here, ye seem to have frightened the poor
man yourself, Leddy Ceecily, by talking to him about the fanatical
Chreestianity of the Americans. Ye have largely yourself to thank
if he's gone.

LADY CICELY. Allah be praised! What a weight off our minds, Mr. Rankin!

RANKIN [*puzzled*]. And why? Do ye not understand how necessary their evidence is?

LADY CICELY. Their evidence! It would spoil everything. They would perjure themselves out of pure spite against poor Captain Brassbound.

RANKIN [*amazed*]. Do ye call him poor Captain Brassbound! Does not your leddyship know that this Brassbound is—Heaven forgive me for judging him!—a precious scoundrel? Did ye not hear what Sir Howrrd told me on the yacht last night?

LADY CICELY. All a mistake, Mr. Rankin: all a mistake, I assure you. You said just now, Heaven forgive you for judging him! Well, that's just what the whole quarrel is about. Captain Brassbound is just like you: he thinks we have no right to judge one another; and its Sir Howard gets £5,000 a year for doing nothing else but judging people, he thinks poor Captain Brassbound a regular Anarchist. They quarreled dreadfully at the castle. You mustn't mind what Sir Howard says about him: you really mustn't.

RANKIN. But his conduct—

LADY CICELY. Perfectly saintly, Mr. Rankin. Worthy of yourself in your best moments. He forgave Sir Howard, and did all he could to save him.

RANKIN. Ye astoanish me, Leddy Ceecily.

LADY CICELY. And think of the temptation to behave badly when he had us all there helpless!

RANKIN. The temptation! ay: that's true. Ye're ower bonny to be cast away among a parcel o lone, lawless men, my leddy.

LADY CICELY [*naively*]. Bless me, that's quite true; and I never thought of it! Oh, after that you really must do all you can to help Captain Brassbound.

RANKIN [*reservedly*]. No: I cannot say that, Leddy Ceecily. I doubt he has imposed on your good nature and sweet disposeetion. I had a crack with the Cadi as well as with Sir Howrrd; and there is little question in my mind but that Captain Brassbound is no better than a breegand.

LADY CICELY [*apparently deeply impressed*]. I wonder whether he can be, Mr. Rankin. If you think so, that's heavily against him in my opinion, because you have more knowledge of men than anyone else here. Perhaps I'm mistaken. I only thought you might like to help him as the son of your old friend.

RANKIN [startled]. The son of my old friend! What d'ye mean?

LADY CICELY. Oh! Didn't Sir Howard tell you that? Why, Captain Brassbound turns out to be Sir Howard's nephew, the son of the brother you knew.

RANKIN [*overwhelmed*]. I saw the likeness the night he came here! It's true: it's true. Uncle and nephew!

LADY CICELY. Yes: that's why they quarrelled so.

RANKIN [*with a momentary sense of ill usage*]. I think Sir Howrrd might have told me that.

LADY CICELY. Of course he ought to have told you. You see he only tells one side of the story. That comes from his training as a barrister. You mustn't think he's naturally deceitful: if he'd been brought up as a clergyman, he'd have told you the whole truth as a matter of course.

RANKIN [*too much perturbed to dwell on his grievance*]. Leddy Ceecily: I must go to the prison and see the lad. He may have been a bit wild; but I can't leave poor Miles's son unbefriended in a foreign gaol.

LADY CICELY [*rising, radiant*]. Oh, how good of you! You have a real kind heart of gold, Mr. Rankin. Now, before you go, shall we just put our heads together, and consider how to give Miles's son every chance—I mean of course every chance that he ought to have.

RANKIN [*rather addled*]. I am so confused by this astoanishing news—

LADY CICELY. Yes, yes: of course you are. But don't you think he would make a better impression on the American captain if he were a little more respectably dressed?

RANKIN. Mebbe. But how can that be remedied here in Mogador?

LADY CICELY. Oh, I've thought of that. You know I'm going back to England by way of Rome, Mr. Rankin; and I'm bringing a portmanteau full of clothes for my brother there: he's ambassador, you know, and has to be very particular as to what he wears. I had the portmanteau brought here this morning. Now would you mind taking it to the prison, and smartening up Captain Brassbound a little. Tell him he ought to do it to show his respect for me; and he will. It will be quite easy: there are two Krooboys waiting to carry the portmanteau. You will: I know you will. [*She edges him to the door.*] And do you think there is time to get him shaved?

RANKIN [*succumbing, half bewildered*]. I'll do my best.

LADY CICELY. I know you will. [*As he is going out*] Oh! one word, Mr. Rankin. [*He comes back.*] The Cadi didn't know that Captain Brassbound was Sir Howard's nephew, did he?

RANKIN. No.

LADY CICELY. Then he must have misunderstood everything quite dreadfully. I'm afraid, Mr. Rankin—though you know best, of course—that we are bound not to repeat anything at the inquiry that the Cadi said. He didn't know, you see.

RANKIN [*cannily*]. I take your point, Leddy Ceecily. It alters the case. I shall certainly make no allusion to it.

LADY CICELY [*magnanimously*]. Well, then, I won't either. There! They shake hands on it. Sir Howard comes in.

SIR HOWARD. Good morning Mr. Rankin. I hope you got home safely from the yacht last night.

RANKIN. Quite safe, thank ye, Sir Howrrd.

LADY CICELY. Howard, he's in a hurry. Don't make him stop to talk.

SIR HOWARD. Very good, very good. [*He comes to the table and takes Lady Cicely's chair.*]

RANKIN. Oo revoir, Leddy Ceecily.

LADY CICELY. Bless you, Mr. Rankin. [*Rankin goes out. She comes to the other end of the table, looking at Sir Howard with a troubled, sorrowfully sympathetic air, but unconsciously making her right hand stalk about the table on the tips of its fingers in a tentative stealthy way which would put Sir Howard on his guard if he were in a suspicious frame of mind, which, as it happens, he is not.*] I'm so sorry for you, Howard, about this unfortunate inquiry.

SIR HOWARD [*swinging round on his chair, astonished*]. Sorry for m e! Why?

LADY CICELY. It will look so dreadful. Your own nephew, you know.

SIR HOWARD. Cicely: an English judge has no nephews, no sons even, when he has to carry out the law.

LADY CICELY. But then he oughtn't to have any property either. People will never understand about the West Indian Estate. They'll think you're the wicked uncle out of the Babes in the Wood. [*With a fresh gush of compassion*] I'm so so sorry for you.

SIR HOWARD [*rather stiffly*]. I really do not see how I need your commiseration, Cicely. The woman was an impossible person, half mad, half drunk. Do you understand what such a creature is when she has a grievance, and imagines some innocent person to be the author of it?

LADY CICELY [*with a touch of impatience*]. Oh, quite. That'll be made clear enough. I can see it all in the papers already: our half mad, half drunk sister-in-law, making scenes with you in the street, with the police called in, and prison and all the rest of it. The family will be furious. [*Sir Howard quails. She instantly follows up her advantage with*] Think of papa!

SIR HOWARD. I shall expect Lord Waynflete to look at the matter as a reasonable man.

LADY CICELY. Do you think he's so greatly changed as that, Howard?

SIR HOWARD [*falling back on the fatalism of the depersonalized public man*]. My dear Cicely: there is no use discussing the matter. It cannot be helped, however disagreeable it may be.

LADY CICELY. Of course not. That's what's so dreadful. Do you think people will understand?

SIR HOWARD. I really cannot say. Whether they do or not, I cannot help it.

LADY CICELY. If you were anybody but a judge, it wouldn't matter so much. But a judge mustn't even be misunderstood. [*Despairingly*] Oh, it's dreadful, Howard: it's terrible! What would poor Mary say if she were alive now?

SIR HOWARD [*with emotion*]. I don't think, Cicely, that my dear wife would misunderstand me.

LADY CICELY. No: she'd know you mean well. And when you came home and said, "Mary: I've just told all the world that your sister-in-law was a police court criminal, and that I sent her to prison; and your nephew is a brigand, and I'm sending him to prison." she'd have thought it must be all right because you did it. But you don't think she would have liked it, any more than papa and the rest of us, do you?

SIR HOWARD [*appalled*]. But what am I to do? Do you ask me to compound a felony?

LADY CICELY [*sternly*]. Certainly not. I would not allow such a thing, even if you were wicked enough to attempt it. No. What I say is, that you ought not to tell the story yourself

SIR HOWARD. Why?

LADY CICELY. Because everybody would say you are such a clever lawyer you could make a poor simple sailor like Captain Kearney believe anything. The proper thing for you to do, Howard, is to let me tell the exact truth. Then you can simply say that you are bound to confirm me. Nobody can blame you for that.

SIR HOWARD [*looking suspiciously at her*]. Cicely: you are up to some devilment.

LADY CICELY [*promptly washing her hands of his interests*]. Oh, very well. Tell the story yourself, in your own clever way. I only proposed to tell the exact truth. You call that devilment. So it is, I daresay, from a lawyer's point of view.

SIR HOWARD. I hope you're not offended.

LADY CICELY [*with the utmost goodhumor*]. My dear Howard, not a bit. Of course you're right: you know how these things ought to be done. I'll do exactly what you tell me, and confirm everything you say.

SIR HOWARD [*alarmed by the completeness of his victory*]. Oh, my dear, you mustn't act in m y interest. You must give your evidence with absolute impartiality. [*She nods, as if thoroughly impressed and reproved, and gazes at him with the steadfast candor peculiar to liars who read novels. His eyes turn to the ground; and his brow clouds perplexedly. He rises; rubs his chin nervously with his forefinger; and adds*] I think, perhaps, on reflection, that there is something to be said for your proposal to relieve me of the very painful duty of telling what has occurred.

LADI CICELY [*holding off*]. But you'd do it so very much better.

SIR HOWARD. For that very reason, perhaps, it had better come from you.

LADY CICELY [*reluctantly*]. Well, if you'd rather.

SIR HOWARD. But mind, Cicely, the exact truth.

LADY CICELY [*with conviction*]. The exact truth. [*They shake hands on it.*]

SIR HOWARD [*holding her hand*]. Fiat justitia: ruat coelum!

LADY CICELY. Let Justice be done, though the ceiling fall.

[*An American bluejacket appears at the door.*]

BLUEJACKET. Captain Kearney's cawmpliments to Lady Waynflete; and may he come in?

LADY CICELY. Yes. By all means. Where are the prisoners?

BLUEJACKET. Party gawn to the jail to fetch em, marm.

LADY CICELY. Thank you. I should like to be told when they are coming, if I might.

BLUEJACKET. You shall so, marm. [*He stands aside, saluting, to admit his captain, and goes out.*]

[*Captain Hamlin Kearney is a robustly built western American, with the keen, squeezed, wind beaten eyes and obstinately enduring mouth of his profession. A curious ethnological specimen, with all the nations of the old world at war in his veins, he is developing artificially in the direction of sleekness and culture under the restraints of an overwhelming dread of European criticism, and climatically in the direction of the indigenous North American, who is already in possession of his hair, his cheekbones, and the manlier instincts in him, which the sea has rescued from civilization. The world, pondering on the great part of its own future which is in his hands, contemplates him with wonder as to what the devil he will evolve into in another century or two. Meanwhile he presents himself to Lady Cicely as a blunt sailor who has something to say to her concerning her conduct which he wishes to put politely, as becomes an officer addressing a lady, but also with an emphatically implied rebuke, as an American addressing an English person who has taken a liberty.*]

LADY CICELY [*as he enters*]. So glad you've come, Captain Kearney.

KEARNEY [*coming between Sir Howard and Lady Cicely*]. When we parted yesterday ahfternoon, Lady Waynflete, I was unaware that in the course of your visit to my ship you had entirely altered the sleeping arrangements of my stokers. I thahnk you. As captain of the ship, I am customairily cawnsulted before the orders of English visitors are carried out; but as your alterations appear to cawndooce to the comfort of the men, I have not interfered with them.

LADY CICELY. How clever of you to find out! I believe you know every bolt in that ship.

[*Kearney softens perceptibly.*]

SIR HOWARD. I am really very sorry that my sister-in-law has taken so serious a liberty, Captain Kearney. It is a mania of hers—simply a mania. Why did your men pay any attention to her?

KEARNEY [*with gravely dissembled humor*]. Well, I ahsked that question too. I said, Why did you obey that lady's orders instead of waiting for mine? They said they didn't see exactly how they could refuse. I ahsked whether they cawnsidered that discipline. They said, Well, sir, will you talk to the lady yourself next time?

LADY CICELY. I'm so sorry. But you know, Captain, the one thing that one misses on board a man-of-war is a woman.

KEARNEY. We often feel that deprivation verry keenly, Lady Waynflete.

LADY CICELY. My uncle is first Lord of the Admiralty; and I am always telling him what a scandal it is that an English captain should be forbidden to take his wife on board to look after the ship.

KEARNEY. Stranger still, Lady Waynflete, he is not forbidden to take any other lady. Yours is an extraordinairy country—to an Amerrican.

LADY CICELY. But it's most serious, Captain. The poor men go melancholy mad, and ram each other's ships and do all sorts of things.

SIR HOWARD. Cicely: I beg you will not talk nonsense to Captain Kearney. Your ideas on some subjects are really hardly decorous.

LADY CICELY [*to Kearney*]. That's what English people are like, Captain Kearney. They won't hear of anything concerning you poor sailors except Nelson and Trafalgar. You understand me, don't you?

KEARNEY [*gallantly*]. I cawnsider that you have more sense in your wedding ring finger than the British Ahdmiralty has in its whole cawnstitootion, Lady Waynflete.

LADY CICELY. Of course I have. Sailors always understand things.

[*The bluejacket reappears.*]

BLUEJACKET [*to Lady Cicely*]. Prisoners coming up the hill, marm.

KEARNEY [*turning sharply on him*]. Who sent you in to say that?

BLUEJACKET [*calmly*]. British lady's orders, sir. [*He goes out, unruffled, leaving Kearney dumbfounded.*]

SIR HOWARD [*contemplating Kearney's expression with dismay*]. I am really very sorry, Captain Kearney. I am quite aware that Lady Cicely has no right whatever to give orders to your men.

LADY CICELY. I didn't give orders: I just asked him. He has such a nice face! Don't you think so, Captain Kearney? [*He gasps, speechless.*] And now will you excuse me a moment. I want to speak to somebody before the inquiry begins. [*She hurries out.*]

KEARNEY. There is sertnly a wonderful chahm about the British aristocracy, Sir Howard Hallam. Are they all like that? [*He takes the presidential chair.*]

SIR HOWARD [*resuming his seat on Kearney's right*]. Fortunately not, Captain Kearney. Half a dozen such women would make an end of law in England in six months.

[*The bluejacket comes to the door again.*]

BLUEJACKET. All ready, sir.

KEARNEY. Verry good. I'm waiting.

[*The bluejacket turns and intimates this to those without. The officers of the Santiago enter.*]

SIR HOWARD [*rising and bobbing to them in a judicial manner*]. Good morning, gentlemen.

[*They acknowledge the greeting rather shyly, bowing or touching their caps, and stand in a group behind Kearney.*]

KEARNEY [*to Sir Howard*]. You will be glahd to hear that I have a verry good account of one of our prisoners from our chahplain, who visited them in the gaol. He has expressed a wish to be cawnverted to Episcopalianism.

SIR HOWARD [*drily*]. Yes, I think I know him.

KEARNEY. Bring in the prisoners.

BLUEJACKET [*at the door*]. They are engaged with the British lady, sir. Shall I ask her—

KEARNEY [*jumping up and exploding in storm piercing tones*]. Bring in the prisoners. Tell the lady those are my orders. Do you hear? Tell her so. [*The bluejacket goes out dubiously. The officers look at one another in mute comment on the unaccountable pepperiness of their commander.*]

SIR HOWARD [*suavely*]. Mr. Rankin will be present, I presume.

KEARNEY [*angrily*]. Rahnkin! Who is Rahnkin?

SIR HOWARD. Our host the missionary.

KEARNEY [*subsiding unwillingly*]. Oh! Rahnkin, is he? He'd better look sharp or he'll be late. [*Again exploding.*] What are they doing with those prisoners?

[*Rankin hurries in, and takes his place near Sir Howard.*]

SIR HOWARD. This is Mr. Rankin, Captain Kearney.

RANKIN. Excuse my delay, Captain Kearney. The leddy sent me on an errand. [*Kearney grunts.*] I thought I should be late. But the first thing I heard when I arrived was your officer giving your compliments to Leddy Ceecily, and would she kindly allow the prisoners to come in, as you were anxious to see her again. Then I knew I was in time.

KEARNEY. Oh, that was it, was it? May I ask, sir, did you notice any sign on Lady Waynflete's part of cawmplying with that verry moderate request?

LADY CICELY [*outside*]. Coming, coming.

[*The prisoners are brought in by a guard of armed bluejackets. Drinkwater first, again elaborately clean, and conveying by a virtuous and steadfast smirk a cheerful confidence in his innocence. Johnson solid and inexpressive, * Redbrook unconcerned and debonair, Marzo uneasy. These four form a little group together on the captain's left. The rest wait unintelligently on Providence in a row against the wall on the same side, shepherded by the bluejackets. The first bluejacket, a petty officer, posts himself on the captain's right, behind Rankin and Sir Howard. Finally Brassbound appears with Lady Cicely on his arm. He is in fashionable frock coat and trousers, spotless collar and cuffs, and elegant boots. He carries a glossy tall hat in his hand. To an unsophisticated eye, the change is monstrous and appalling; and its effect on himself is so unmanning that he is quite out of countenance—a shaven Samson. Lady Cicely, however, is greatly pleased with it; and the rest regard it as an unquestionable improvement. The officers fall back gallantly to allow her to pass. Kearney rises to receive her, and stares with some surprise at Brassbound as he stops at the table on his left. Sir Howard rises punctiliously when Kearney rises and sits when he sits.*]

KEARNEY. Is this another gentleman of your party, Lady Waynflete? I presume I met you lahst night, sir, on board the yacht.

BRASSBOUND. No. I am your prisoner. My name is Brassbound.

DRINKWATER [*officiously*]. Kepn Brarsbahnd, of the schooner Thenksgiv—

REDBROOK [*hastily*]. Shut up, you fool. [*He elbows Drinkwater into the background.*]

KEARNEY [*surprised and rather suspicious*]. Well, I hardly understahnd this. However, if you are Captain Brassbound, you can take your place with the rest. [*Brassbound joins Redbrook and Johnson. Kearney sits down again, after inviting Lady Cicely, with a solemn gesture, to take the vacant chair.*] Now let me see. You are a man of experience in these matters, Sir Howard Hallam. If you had to conduct this business, how would you start?

LADY CICELY. He'd call on the counsel for the prosecution, wouldn't you, Howard?

SIR HOWARD. But there is no counsel for the prosecution, Cicely.

LADY CICELY. Oh yes there is. I'm counsel for the prosecution. You mustn't let Sir Howard make a speech, Captain Kearney: his doctors have positively forbidden anything of that sort. Will you begin with me?

KEARNEY. By your leave, Lady Waynflete, I think I will just begin with myself. Sailor fashion will do as well here as lawyer fashion.

LADY CICELY. Ever so much better, dear Captain Kearney. [*Silence. Kearney composes himself to speak. She breaks out again*]. You look so nice as a judge!

[*A general smile. Drinkwater splutters into a half suppressed laugh.*]

REDBROOK [*in a fierce whisper*]. Shut up, you fool, will you? [*Again he pushes him back with a furtive kick.*]

SIR HOWARD [*remonstrating*]. Cicely!

KEARNEY [*grimly keeping his countenance*]. Your ladyship's cawmpliments will be in order at a later stage. Captain Brassbound: the position is this. My ship, the United States cruiser Santiago, was spoken off Mogador latest Thursday by the yacht Redgauntlet. The owner of the aforesaid yacht, who is not present through having sprained his ankle, gave me sertn information. In cawnsequence of that information the Santiago made the twenty knots to Mogador Harbor inside of fifty-seven minutes. Before noon next day a messenger of mine gave the Cadi of the district sertn information. In cawnsequence of that information the Cadi stimulated himself to some ten knots an hour, and lodged you and your men in Mogador jail at my disposal. The Cadi then went back to his mountain fahstnesses; so we shall not have the pleasure of his company here to-day. Do you follow me so far?

BRASSBOUND. Yes. I know what you did and what the Cadi did. The point is, why did you do it?

KEARNEY. With doo patience we shall come to that presently. Mr. Rahnkin: will you kindly take up the parable?

RANKIN. On the very day that Sir Howrrd and Lady Cicely started on their excursion I was applied to for medicine by a follower of the Sheikh Sidi el Assif. He told me I should never see Sir Howrrd again, because his master knew he was a Christian and would take him out of the hands of Captain Brassbound. I hurried on board the yacht and told the owner to scour the coast for a gunboat or cruiser to come into the harbor and put persuasion on the authorities. [*Sir Howard turns and looks at Rankin with a sudden doubt of his integrity as a witness.*]

KEARNEY. But I understood from our chahplain that you reported Captain Brassbound as in league with the Sheikh to deliver Sir Howard up to him.

RANKIN. That was my first hasty conclusion, Captain Kearney. But it appears that the compact between them was that Captain Brassbound should escort travellers under the Sheikh's protection at a certain payment per head, provided none of them were Christians. As I understand it, he tried to smuggle Sir Howrrd through under this compact, and the Sheikh found him out.

DRINKWATER. Rawt, gavner. Thet's jest ah it wors. The Kepn—

REDBROOK [*again suppressing him*]. Shut up, you fool, I tell you.

SIR HOWARD [*to Rankin*]. May I ask have you had any conversation with Lady Cicely on this subject?

RANKIN [*naively*]. Yes. [*Sir Howard grunts emphatically, as who should say "I thought so." Rankin continues, addressing the court*] May I say how sorry I am that there are so few chairs, Captain and gentlemen.

KEARNEY [*with genial American courtesy*]. Oh, that's all right, Mr. Rahnkin. Well, I see no harm so far: it's human fawlly, but not human crime. Now the counsel for the prosecution can proceed to prosecute. The floor is yours, Lady Waynflete.

LADY CICELY [*rising*]. I can only tell you the exact truth—

DRINKWATER [*involuntarily*]. Naow, down't do thet, lidy—

REDBROOK [*as before*]. Shut up, you fool, will you?

LADY CICELY. We had a most delightful trip in the hills; and Captain Brassbound's men could not have been nicer—I must say that for them—until we saw a tribe of Arabs—such nice looking men!—and then the poor things were frightened.

KEARNEY. The Arabs?

LADY CICELY. No: Arabs are never frightened. The escort, of course: escorts are always frightened. I wanted to speak to the Arab chief; but Captain Brassbound cruelly shot his horse; and the chief shot the Count; and then—

KEARNEY. The Count! What Count?

LADY CICELY. Marzo. That's Marzo [*pointing to Marzo, who grins and touches his forehead*].

KEARNEY [*slightly overwhelmed by the unexpected profusion of incident and character in her story*]. Well, what happened then?

LADY CICELY. Then the escort ran away—all escorts do—and dragged me into the castle, which you really ought to make them clean and whitewash thoroughly, Captain Kearney. Then Captain Brassbound and Sir Howard turned out to be related to one another [sensation]; and then of course, there was a quarrel. The Hallams always quarrel.

SIR HOWARD [*rising to protest*]. Cicely! Captain Kearney: this man told me—

LADY CICELY [*swiftly interrupting him*]. You mustn't say what people told you: it's not evidence. [*Sir Howard chokes with indignation.*]

KEARNEY [*calmly*]. Allow the lady to proceed, Sir Howard Hallam.

SIR HOWARD [*recovering his self-control with a gulp, and resuming his seat*]. I beg your pardon, Captain Kearney.

LADY CICELY. Then Sidi came.

KEARNEY. Sidney! Who was Sidney?

LADY CICELY. No, Sidi. The Sheikh. Sidi el Assif. A noble creature, with such a fine face! He fell in love with me at first sight—

SIR HOWARD [*remonstrating*]. Cicely!

LADY CICELY. He did: you know he did. You told me to tell the exact truth.

KEARNEY. I can readily believe it, madam. Proceed.

LADY CICELY. Well, that put the poor fellow into a most cruel dilemma. You see, he could claim to carry off Sir Howard, because Sir Howard is a Christian. But as I am only a woman, he had no claim to me.

KEARNEY [*somewhat sternly, suspecting Lady Cicely of aristocratic atheism*]. But you are a Christian woman.

LADY CICELY. No: the Arabs don't count women. They don't believe we have any souls.

RANKIN. That is true, Captain: the poor benighted creatures!

LADY CICELY. Well, what was he to do? He wasn't in love with Sir Howard; and he WAS in love with me. So he naturally offered to swop Sir Howard for me. Don't you think that was nice of him, Captain Kearney?

KEARNEY. I should have done the same myself, Lady Waynflete. Proceed.

LADY CICELY. Captain Brassbound, I must say, was nobleness itself, in spite of the quarrel between himself and Sir Howard. He refused to give up either of us, and was on the point of fighting for us when in came the Cadi with your most amusing and delightful letter, captain, and bundled us all back to Mogador after calling my poor Sidi the most dreadful names, and putting all the blame on Captain Brassbound. So here we are. Now, Howard, isn't that the exact truth, every word of it?

SIR HOWARD. It is the truth, Cicely, and nothing but the truth. But the English law requires a witness to tell the whole truth.

LADY CICELY. What nonsense! As if anybody ever knew the whole truth about anything! [*Sitting down, much hurt and discouraged.*] I'm sorry you wish Captain Kearney to understand that I am an untruthful witness.

SIR HOWARD. No: but—

LADY CICELY. Very well, then: please don't say things that convey that impression.

KEARNEY. But Sir Howard told me yesterday that Captain Brassbound threatened to sell him into slavery.

LADY CICELY [*springing up again*]. Did Sir Howard tell you the things he said about Captain Brassbound's mother? [*Renewed sensation.*] I told you they quarrelled, Captain Kearney. I said so, didn't I?

REDBROOK [*crisply*]. Distinctly. [*Drinkwater opens his mouth to corroborate.*] Shut up, you fool.

LADY CICELY. Of course I did. Now, Captain Kearney, do you want me—does Sir Howard want me—does anybody want me to go into the details of that shocking family quarrel? Am I to stand here in the absence of any individual of my own sex and repeat the language of two angry men?

KEARNEY [*rising impressively*]. The United States navy will have no hahnd in offering any violence to the pure instincts of womanhood. Lady Waynflete: I thahnk you for the delicacy with which you have given your evidence. [*Lady Cicely beams on him gratefully and sits down triumphant.*] Captain Brassbound: I shall not hold you respawnsible for what you may have said when the English

bench addressed you in the language of the English forecastle—
[*Sir Howard is about to protest.*] No, Sir Howard Hallam: excuse
m e. In moments of pahssion I have called a man that myself. We
are glahd to find real flesh and blood beneath the ermine of the
judge. We will all now drop a subject that should never have been
broached in a lady's presence. [*He resumes his seat, and adds, in a
businesslike tone*] Is there anything further before we release these
men?

BLUEJACKET. There are some dawcuments handed over by the Cadi,
sir. He reckoned they were sort of magic spells. The chahplain
ordered them to be reported to you and burnt, with your leave, sir.

KEARNEY. What are they?

BLUEJACKET [*reading from a list*]. Four books, torn and dirty, made
up of separate numbers, value each wawn penny, and entitled
Sweeny Todd, the Demon Barber of London; The Skeleton
Horseman—

DRINKWATER [*rushing forward in painful alarm, and anxiety*]. It's
maw lawbrary, gavner. Down't burn em.

KEARNEY. You'll be better without that sort of reading, my man.

DRINKWATER [*in intense distress, appealing to Lady Cicely*] Down't
let em burn em, Lidy. They dassent if you horder them not to.
[*With desperate eloquence*] Yer dunno wot them books is to me.
They took me aht of the sawdid reeyellities of the Worterleoo
Rowd. They formed maw mawnd: they shaowed me sathink
awgher than the squalor of a corster's lawf—

REDBROOK [*collaring him*]. Oh shut up, you fool. Get out. Hold your
ton—

DRINKWATER [*frantically breaking from him*]. Lidy, lidy: sy a word
for me. Ev a feelin awt. [*His tears choke him: he clasps his hands
in dumb entreaty.*]

LADY CICELY [*touched*]. Don't burn his books. Captain. Let me give
them back to him.

KEARNEY. The books will be handed over to the lady.

DRINKWATER [*in a small voice*]. Thenkyer, Lidy. [*He retires among
his comrades, snivelling subduedly.*]

REDBROOK [*aside to him as he passes*]. You silly ass, you.
[*Drinkwater sniffs and does not reply.*]

KEARNEY. I suppose you and your men accept this lady's account of
what passed, Captain Brassbound.

BRASSBOUND [*gloomily*]. Yes. It is true—as far as it goes.

KEARNEY [*impatiently*]. Do you wawnt it to go any further?

MARZO. She leave out something. Arab shoot me. She nurse me. She cure me.

KEARNEY. And who are you, pray?

MARZO [*seized with a sanctimonious desire to demonstrate his higher nature*]. Only dam thief. Dam liar. Dam rascal. She no lady.

JOHNSON [*revolted by the seeming insult to the English peerage from a low Italian*]. What? What's that you say?

MARZO. No lady nurse dam rascal. Only saint. She saint. She get me to heaven—get us all to heaven. We do what we like now.

LADY CICELY. Indeed you will do nothing of the sort Marzo, unless you like to behave yourself very nicely indeed. What hour did you say we were to lunch at, Captain Kearney?

KEARNEY. You recall me to my dooty, Lady Waynflete. My barge will be ready to take off you and Sir Howard to the Santiago at one o'clawk. [*He rises.*] Captain Brassbound: this innquery has elicited no reason why I should detain you or your men. I advise you to ahct as escort in future to heathens exclusively. Mr. Rahnkin: I thahnk you in the name of the United States for the hospitahlity you have extended to us today; and I invite you to accompany me bahck to my ship with a view to lunch at half-past one. Gentlemen: we will wait on the governor of the gaol on our way to the harbor [*He goes out, following his officers, and followed by the bluejackets and the petty officer.*]

SIR HOWARD [*to Lady Cicely*]. Cicely: in the course of my professional career I have met with unscrupulous witnesses, and, I am sorry to say, unscrupulous counsel also. But the combination of unscrupulous witness and unscrupulous counsel I have met to-day has taken away my breath You have made me your accomplice in defeating justice.

LADY CICELY. Yes: aren't you glad it's been defeated for once? [*She takes his arm to go out with him.*] Captain Brassbound: I will come back to say goodbye before I go. [*He nods gloomily. She goes out with Sir Howard, following the Captain and his staff.*]

RANKIN [*running to Brassbound and taking both his hands*]. I'm right glad yere cleared. I'll come back and have a crack with ye when yon lunch is over. God bless ye. [*Hs goes out quickly.*]

[*Brassbound and his men, left by themselves in the room, free and unobserved, go straight out of their senses. They laugh; they dance; they embrace one another; they set to partners and waltz clumsily; they shake hands repeatedly and maudlinly. Three only retain some sort of self-possession. Marzo, proud*] *of having successfully thrust himself into a leading part in the recent proceedings and made a dramatic speech, inflates his chest, curls his scanty moustache, and throws himself into a swaggering pose, chin up and right foot forward, despising the emotional English barbarians around him. Brassbound's eyes and the working of his mouth show that he is infected with the general excitement; but he bridles himself savagely. Redbrook, trained to affect indifference, grins cynically; winks at Brassbound; and finally relieves himself by assuming the character of a circus ringmaster, flourishing an imaginary whip and egging on the rest to wilder exertions. A climax is reached when Drinkwater, let loose without a stain on his character for the second time, is rapt by belief in his star into an ecstasy in which, scorning all partnership, he becomes as it were a whirling dervish, and executes so miraculous a clog dance that the others gradually cease their slower antics to stare at him.]*

BRASSBOUND [*tearing off his hat and striding forward as Drinkwater collapses, exhausted, and is picked up by Redbrook*]. Now to get rid of this respectable clobber and feel like a man again. Stand by, all hands, to jump on the captain's tall hat. [*He puts the hat down and prepares to jump on it. The effect is startling, and takes him completely aback. His followers, far from appreciating his iconoclasm, are shocked into scandalized sobriety, except Redbrook, who is immensely tickled by their prudery.*]

DRINKWATER. Naow, look eah, kepn: that ynt rawt. Dror a lawn somewhere.

JOHNSON. I say nothin agen a bit of fun, Capn, but let's be gentlemen.

REDBROOK. I suggest to you, Brassbound, that the clobber belongs to Lady Sis. Ain't you going to give it back to her?

BRASSBOUND [*picking up the hat and brushing the dust off it anxiously*]. That's true. I'm a fool. All the same, she shall not see me again like this. [*He pulls off the coat and waistcoat together.*] Does any man here know how to fold up this sort of thing properly?

REDBROOK. Allow me, governor. [*He takes the coat and waistcoat to the table, and folds them up.*]

BRASSBOUND [*loosening his collar and the front of his shirt*]. Brandyfaced Jack: you're looking at these studs. I know what's in your mind.

DRINKWATER [*indignantly*]. Naow yer down't: nort a bit on it. Wot's in maw mawnd is secrifawce, seolf-secrifawce.

BRASSBOUND. If one brass pin of that lady's property is missing, I'll hang you with my own hands at the gaff of the Thanksgiving—and would, if she were lying under the guns of all the fleets in Europe. [*He pulls off the shirt and stands in his blue jersey, with his hair ruffled. He passes his hand through it and exclaims*] Now I am half a man, at any rate.

REDBROOK. A horrible combination, governor: churchwarden from the waist down, and the rest pirate. Lady Sis won't speak to you in it.

BRASSBOUND. I'll change altogether. [*He leaves the room to get his own trousers.*]

REDBROOK [*softly*]. Look here, Johnson, and gents generally. [*They gather about him.*] Spose she takes him back to England!

MARZO [*trying to repeat his success*]. Im! Im only dam pirate. She saint, I tell you—no take any man nowhere.

JOHNSON [*severely*]. Don't you be a ignorant and immoral foreigner. [*The rebuke is well received; and Marzo is hustled into the background and extinguished.*] She won't take him for harm; but she might take him for good. And then where should we be?

DRINKWATER. Brarsbahnd ynt the ownly kepn in the world. Wot mikes a kepn is brines an knollidge o lawf. It ynt thet ther's naow sitch pusson: it's thet you dunno where to look fr im. [*The implication that he is such a person is so intolerable that they receive it with a prolonged burst of booing.*]

BRASSBOUND [*returning in his own clothes, getting into his jacket as he comes*]. Stand by, all. [*They start asunder guiltily, and wait for orders.*] Redbrook: you pack that clobber in the lady's portmanteau, and put it aboard the yacht for her. Johnson: you take all hands aboard the Thanksgiving; look through the stores: weigh anchor; and make all ready for sea. Then send Jack to wait for me at the slip with a boat; and give me a gunfire for a signal. Lose no time.

JOHNSON. Ay, ay, air. All aboard, mates.

ALL. Ay, ay. [*They rush out tumultuously.*]

[*When they are gone, Brassbound sits down at the end of the table, with his elbows on it and his head on his fists, gloomily thinking. Then he takes from the breast pocket of his jacket a leather case, from which he extracts a scrappy packet of dirty letters and newspaper cuttings. These he throws on the table.*

Next comes a photograph in a cheap frame. He throws it down untenderly beside the papers; then folds his arms, and is looking at it with grim distaste when Lady Cicely enters. His back is towards her; and he does not hear her. Perceiving this, she shuts the door loudly enough to attract his attention. He starts up.]

LADY CICELY [*coming to the opposite end of the table*]. So you've taken off all my beautiful clothes!

BRASSBOUND. Your brother's, you mean. A man should wear his own clothes; and a man should tell his own lies. I'm sorry you had to tell mine for me to-day.

LADY CICELY. Oh, women spend half their lives telling little lies for men, and sometimes big ones. We're used to it. But mind! I don't admit that I told any to-day.

BRASSBOUND. How did you square my uncle?

LADY CICELY. I don't understand the expression.

BRASSBOUND. I mean—

LADY CICELY. I'm afraid we haven't time to go into what you mean before lunch. I want to speak to you about your future. May I?

BRASSBOUND [*darkening a little, but politely*]. Sit down. [*She sits down. So does he.*]

LADY CICELY. What are your plans?

BRASSBOUND. I have no plans. You will hear a gun fired in the harbor presently. That will mean that the Thanksgiving's anchor's weighed and that she is waiting for her captain to put out to sea. And her captain doesn't know now whether to turn her head north or south.

LADY CICELY. Why not north for England?

BRASSBOUND. Why not south for the Pole?

LADY CICELY. But you must do something with yourself.

BRASSBOUND [*settling himself with his fists and elbows weightily on the table and looking straight and powerfully at her*]. Look you: when you and I first met, I was a man with a purpose. I stood alone: I saddled no friend, woman or man, with that purpose, because it was against law, against religion, against my own credit and safety. But I believed in it; and I stood alone for it, as a man should stand for his belief, against law and religion as much as against wickedness and selfishness. Whatever I may be, I am none of your fair-weather sailors that'll do nothing for their creed but go to Heaven for it. I was ready to go to hell for mine. Perhaps you don't understand that.

LADY CICELY. Oh bless you, yes. It's so very like a certain sort of man.

BRASSBOUND. I daresay but I've not met many of that sort. Anyhow, that was what I was like. I don't say I was happy in it; but I wasn't unhappy, because I wasn't drifting. I was steering a course and had work in hand. Give a man health and a course to steer; and he'll never stop to trouble about whether he's happy or not.

LADY CICELY. Sometimes he won't even stop to trouble about whether other people are happy or not.

BRASSBOUND. I don't deny that: nothing makes a man so selfish as work. But I was not self-seeking: it seemed to me that I had put justice above self. I tell you life meant something to me then. Do you see that dirty little bundle of scraps of paper?

LADY CICELY. What are they?

BRASSBOUND. Accounts cut out of newspapers. Speeches made by my uncle at charitable dinners, or sentencing men to death—pious, high-minded speeches by a man who was to me a thief and a murderer! To my mind they were more weighty, more momentous, better revelations of the wickedness of law and respectability than the book of the prophet Amos. What are they now? [*He quietly tears the newspaper cuttings into little fragments and throws them away, looking fixedly at her meanwhile.*]

LADY CICELY. Well, that's a comfort, at all events.

BRASSBOUND. Yes; but it's a part of my life gone: your doing, remember. What have I left? See here! [*He take up the letters*] the letters my uncle wrote to my mother, with her comments on their cold drawn insolence, their treachery and cruelty. And the piteous letters she wrote to him later on, returned unopened. Must they go too?

LADY CICELY [*uneasily*]. I can't ask you to destroy your mother's letters.

BRASSBOUND. Why not, now that you have taken the meaning out of them? [*He tears them.*] Is that a comfort too?

LADY CICELY. It's a little sad; but perhaps it is best so.

BRASSBOUND. That leaves one relic: her portrait. [*He plucks the photograph out of its cheap case.*]

LADY CICELY [*with vivid curiosity*]. Oh, let me see. [*He hands it to her. Before she can control herself, her expression changes to one of unmistakable disappointment and repulsion.*]

BRASSBOUND [*with a single sardonic cachinnation*]. Ha! You expected something better than that. Well, you're right. Her face does not look well opposite yours.

LADY CICELY [*distressed*]. I said nothing.

BRASSBOUND. What could you say? [He takes back the portrait: she relinquishes it without a word. He looks at it; shakes his head; and takes it quietly between his finger and thumb to tear it.]

LADY CICELY [*staying his hand*]. Oh, not your mother's picture!

BRASSBOUND. If that were your picture, would you like your son to keep it for younger and better women to see?

LADY CICELY [*releasing his hand*]. Oh, you are dreadful! Tear it, tear it. [She covers her eyes for a moment to shut out the sight.]

BRASSBOUND [*tearing it quietly*]. You killed her for me that day in the castle; and I am better without her. [*He throws away the fragments.*] Now everything is gone. You have taken the old meaning out of my life; but you have put no new meaning into it. I can see that you have some clue to the world that makes all its difficulties easy for you; but I'm not clever enough to seize it. You've lamed me by showing me that I take life the wrong way when I'm left to myself.

LADY CICELY. Oh no. Why do you say that?

BRASSBOUND. What else can I say? See what I've done! My uncle is no worse a man than myself—better, most likely; for he has a better head and a higher place. Well, I took him for a villain out of a storybook. My mother would have opened anybody else's eyes: she shut mine. I'm a stupider man than Brandyfaced Jack even; for he got his romantic nonsense out of his penny numbers and such like trash; but I got just the same nonsense out of life and experience. [*Shaking his head*] It was vulgar—vulgar. I see that now; for you've opened my eyes to the past; but what good is that for the future? What am I to do? Where am I to go?

LADY CICELY. It's quite simple. Do whatever you like. That's what I always do.

BRASSBOUND. That answer is no good to me. What I like is to have something to do; and I have nothing. You might as well talk like the missionary and tell me to do my duty.

LADY CICELY [*quickly*]. Oh no thank you. I've had quite enough of your duty, and Howard's duty. Where would you both be now if I'd let you do it?

BRASSBOUND. We'd have been somewhere, at all events. It seems to me that now I am nowhere.

LADY CICELY. But aren't you coming back to England with us?

BRASSBOUND. What for?

LADY CICELY. Why, to make the most of your opportunities.

BRASSBOUND. What opportunities?

LADY CICELY. Don't you understand that when you are the nephew of a great bigwig, and have influential connexions, and good friends among them, lots of things can be done for you that are never done for ordinary ship captains?

BRASSBOUND. Ah; but I'm not an aristocrat, you see. And like most poor men, I'm proud. I don't like being patronized.

LADY CICELY. What is the use of saying that? In my world, which is now your world—our world—getting patronage is the whole art of life. A man can't have a career without it.

BRASSBOUND. In my world a man can navigate a ship and get his living by it.

LADY CICELY. Oh, I see you're one of the Idealists—the Impossibilists! We have them, too, occasionally, in our world. There's only one thing to be done with them.

BRASSBOUND. What's that?

LADY CICELY. Marry them straight off to some girl with enough money for them, and plenty of sentiment. That's their fate.

BRASSBOUND. You've spoiled even that chance for me. Do you think I could look at any ordinary woman after you? You seem to be able to make me do pretty well what you like; but you can't make me marry anybody but yourself.

LADY CICELY. Do you know, Captain Paquito, that I've married no less than seventeen men [*Brassbound stares*] to other women. And they all opened the subject by saying that they would never marry anybody but me.

BRASSBOUND. Then I shall be the first man you ever found to stand to his word.

LADY CICELY [*part pleased, part amused, part sympathetic*]. Do you really want a wife?

BRASSBOUND. I want a commander. Don't undervalue me: I am a good man when I have a good leader. I have courage: I have determination: I'm not a drinker: I can command a schooner and a shore party if I can't command a ship or an army. When work is put upon me, I turn neither to save my life nor to fill my pocket. Gordon trusted me; and he never regretted it. If you trust me, you shan't regret it. All the same, there's something wanting in me: I suppose I'm stupid.

LADY CICELY. Oh, you're not stupid.

BRASSBOUND. Yes I am. Since you saw me for the first time in that garden, you've heard me say nothing clever. And I've heard you say nothing that didn't make me laugh, or make me feel friendly, as well as telling me what to think and what to do. That's what I mean by real cleverness. Well, I haven't got it. I can give an order when I know what order to give. I can make men obey it, willing or unwilling. But I'm stupid, I tell you: stupid. When there's no Gordon to command me, I can't think of what to do. Left to myself, I've become half a brigand. I can kick that little gutterscrub Drinkwater; but I find myself doing what he puts into my head because I can't think of anything else. When you came, I took your orders as naturally as I took Gordon's, though I little thought my next commander would be a woman. I want to take service under you. And there's no way in which that can be done except marrying you. Will you let me do it?

LADY CICELY. I'm afraid you don't quite know how odd a match it would be for me according to the ideas of English society.

BRASSBOUND. I care nothing about English society: let it mind its own business.

LADY CICELY [*rising, a little alarmed*]. Captain Paquito: I am not in love with you.

BRASSBOUND [*also rising, with his gaze still steadfastly on her*]. I didn't suppose you were: the commander is not usually in love with his subordinate.

LADY CICELY. Nor the subordinate with the commander.

BRASSBOUND [*assenting firmly*]. Nor the subordinate with the commander.

LADY CICELY [*learning for the first time in her life what terror is, as she finds that he is unconsciously mesmerizing her*]. Oh, you are dangerous!

BRASSBOUND. Come: are you in love with anybody else? That's the question.

LADY CICELY [*shaking her head*]. I have never been in love with any real person; and I never shall. How could I manage people if I had that mad little bit of self left in me? That's my secret.

BRASSBOUND. Then throw away the last bit of self. Marry me.

LADY CICELY [*vainly struggling to recall her wandering will*]. Must I?

BRASSBOUND. There is no must. You can. I ask you to. My fate depends on it.

LADY CICELY. It's frightful; for I don't mean to—don't wish to.

BRASSBOUND. But you will.

LADY CICELY [*quite lost, slowly stretches out her hand to give it to him*]. I— [*Gunfire from the Thanksgiving. His eyes dilate. It wakes her from her trance*] What is that?

BRASSBOUND. It is farewell. Rescue for you—safety, freedom! You were made to be something better than the wife of Black Paquito. [*He kneels and takes her hands*] You can do no more for me now: I have blundered somehow on the secret of command at last [*he kisses her hands*]: thanks for that, and for a man's power and purpose restored and righted. And farewell, farewell, farewell.

LADY CICELY [*in a strange ecstasy, holding his hands as he rises*]. Oh, farewell. With my heart's deepest feeling, farewell, farewell.

BRASSBOUND. With my heart's noblest honor and triumph, farewell. [*He turns and flies.*]

LADY CICELY. How glorious! how glorious! And what an escape!

CURTAIN

NOTES TO CAPTAIN BRASSBOUND'S CONVERSION

SOURCES OF THE PLAY

I claim as a notable merit in the authorship of this play that I have been intelligent enough to steal its scenery, its surroundings, its atmosphere, its geography, its knowledge of the east, its fascinating Cadis and Kearneys and Sheikhs and mud castles from an excellent book of philosophic travel and vivid adventure entitled Mogreb-el-Acksa (Morocco the Most Holy) by Cunninghame Graham. My own first hand knowledge of Morocco is based on a morning's walk through Tangier, and a cursory observation of the coast through a binocular from the deck of an Orient steamer, both later in date than the writing of the play.

Cunninghame Graham is the hero of his own book; but I have not made him the hero of my play, because so incredible a personage must have destroyed its likelihood—such as it is. There are moments when I do not myself believe in his existence. And yet he must be real; for I have seen him with these eyes; and I am one of the few men living who can decipher the curious alphabet in which he writes his private letters. The man is on public record too. The battle of Trafalgar Square, in which he personally and bodily assailed civilization as represented by the concentrated military and constabular forces of the capital of the world, can scarcely be forgotten by the more discreet spectators, of whom I was one. On that occasion civilization, qualitatively his inferior, was quantitatively so hugely in excess of him that it put him in prison, but had not sense enough to keep him there. Yet his getting out of prison was as nothing compared to his getting into the House of Commons. How he did it I know not; but the thing certainly happened, somehow. That he made pregnant utterances as a legislator may be taken as proved by the keen philosophy of the travels and tales he has since tossed to us; but the House, strong in stupidity, did not understand him until in an inspired moment he voiced a universal impulse by bluntly damning its hypocrisy. Of all the eloquence of that silly parliament, there remains only one single damn. It has survived the front bench speeches of the eighties as the word of Cervantes survives the oraculations of the Dons and Deys who put him, too, in prison. The shocked House demanded that he should withdraw his cruel word. "I never withdraw," said he; and I promptly stole the potent phrase for the sake of its perfect style, and used it as a cockade for the Bulgarian hero of Arms and the Man. The theft prospered; and I naturally take the first opportunity of repeating it. In what other Lepantos besides Trafalgar Square Cunninghame Graham has fought, I cannot tell. He is a fascinating mystery to a sedentary person like myself. The horse, a dangerous animal whom, when I cannot avoid, I propitiate with apples and sugar, he bestrides and dominates fearlessly, yet with a true republican sense of the rights of the four legged fellow creature whose martyrdom, and man's shame therein, he has told most powerfully in his Calvary, a tale with an edge that will cut the soft cruel hearts and strike fire from the hard kind ones. He handles the other lethal weapons as familiarly as the pen: medieval sword and modern Mauser are to him as umbrellas and kodaks are to me. His tales of adventure have the true Cervantes touch of the man who has been there—so refreshingly different from the scenes imagined by bloody-minded clerks who escape from their servitude into literature to tell us how men and cities are conceived in the counting house and the volunteer corps. He is, I understand, a Spanish hidalgo: hence the superbity of his portrait by Lavery (Velasquez being no longer available). He is, I know, a Scotch laird. How he contrives to be authentically the two things at the same time is no more intelligible to me than the fact that everything that has ever happened to him seems to have happened in Paraguay or Texas instead of in Spain or Scotland. He is, I regret to add, an impenitent and unashamed dandy: such boots, such a hat, would have dazzled D'Orsay himself. With that hat he once saluted me in Regent St. when I was walking with my mother. Her interest was instantly kindled; and the following conversation ensued. "Who is that?" "Cunninghame Graham." "Nonsense! Cunninghame Graham is one of your Socialists: that man is a gentleman." This is the punishment of vanity, a fault I have myself always avoided, as I find conceit less troublesome and much less expensive. Later on somebody told him of Tarudant, a city in Morocco in which no Christian had ever set foot. Concluding at once that it must be an exceptionally desirable place to live in, he took ship and horse: changed the hat for a turban; and made straight for the sacred city, via Mogador. How he fared, and how he fell into the hands of the Cadi of Kintafi, who rightly held that there was more danger to Islam in one Cunninghame Graham than in a thousand Christians, may be learnt from his account of it in Mogreb-el-Acksa, without which Captain Brassbound's Conversion would never have been written.

I am equally guiltless of any exercise of invention concerning the story of the West Indian estate which so very nearly serves as a peg to hang Captain Brassbound. To Mr. Frederick Jackson of Hind head, who, against all his principles, encourages and abets me in my career as a dramatist, I owe my knowledge of those main facts of the case which became public through an attempt to make the House of Commons act on them. This being so, I must add that the character of Captain Brassbound's mother, like the recovery of the estate by the next heir, is an interpolation of my own. It is not, however, an invention. One of the evils of the pretence that our institutions represent abstract principles of justice instead of being mere social scaffolding is that persons of a certain temperament take the pretence seriously, and when the law is on the side of injustice, will not accept the situation, and are driven mad by their vain struggle against it. Dickens has drawn the type in his Man from Shropshire in Bleak House. Most public men and all lawyers have been appealed to by victims of this sense of injustice—the most unhelpable of afflictions in a society like ours.

ENGLISH AND AMERICAN DIALECTS

The fact that English is spelt conventionally and not phonetically makes the art of recording speech almost impossible. What is more, it places the modern dramatist, who writes for America as well as England, in a most trying position. Take for example my American captain and my English lady. I have spelt the word conduce, as uttered by the American captain, as cawndooce, to suggest [very roughly] the American pronunciation to English readers. Then why not spell the same word, when uttered by Lady Cicely, as kerndewce, to suggest the English pronunciation to American readers? To this I have absolutely no defence: I can only plead that an author who lives in England necessarily loses his consciousness of the peculiarities of English speech, and sharpens his consciousness of the points in which American speech differs from it; so that it is more convenient to leave English peculiarities to be recorded by American authors. I must, however, most vehemently disclaim any intention of suggesting that English pronunciation is authoritative and correct. My own tongue is neither American English nor English English, but Irish English; so I am as nearly impartial in the matter as it is in human nature to be. Besides, there is no standard English pronunciation any more than there is an American one: in England every county has its catchwords, just as no doubt every state in the Union has. I cannot believe that the pioneer American, for example, can spare time to learn that last refinement of modern speech, the exquisite diphthong, a farfetched combination of the French eu and the English e, with which a New Yorker pronounces such words as world, bird &c. I have spent months without success in trying to achieve glibness with it.

To Felix Drinkwater also I owe some apology for implying that all his vowel pronunciations are unfashionable. They are very far from being so. As far as my social experience goes (and I have kept very mixed company) there is no class in English society in which a good deal of Drinkwater pronunciation does not pass unchallenged save by the expert phonetician. This is no mere rash and ignorant jibe of my own at the expense of my English neighbors. Academic authority in the matter of English speech is represented at present by Mr. Henry Sweet, of the University of Oxford, whose *Elementarbuch des gesprochenen Englisch*, translated into his native language for the use of British islanders as a Primer of Spoken English, is the most accessible standard work on the subject. In such words as plum, come, humbug, up, gum, etc., Mr. Sweet's evidence is conclusive. Ladies and gentlemen in Southern England pronounce them as plam, kam, hambag, ap, gan, etc., exactly as Felix Drinkwater does. I could not claim Mr. Sweet's authority if I dared to whisper that such coster English as the rather pretty dahn tahn for down town, or the decidedly ugly cowcow for cocoa is current in very polite circles. The entire nation, costers and all, would undoubtedly repudiate any such pronunciation as vulgar. All the same, if I were to attempt to represent current "smart" cockney speech as I have attempted to represent Drinkwater's, without the niceties of Mr. Sweet's Romic alphabets, I am afraid I should often have to write dahn tahn and cowcow as being at least nearer to the actual sound than down town and cocoa. And this would give such offence that I should have to leave the country; for nothing annoys a native speaker of English more than a faithful setting down in phonetic spelling of the sounds he utters. He imagines that a departure from conventional spelling indicates a departure from the correct standard English of good society. Alas! this correct standard English of good society is unknown to phoneticians. It is only one of the many figments that bewilder our poor snobbish brains. No such thing exists; but what does that matter to people trained from infancy to make a point of honor of belief in abstractions and incredibilities? And so I am compelled to hide Lady Cicely's speech under the veil of conventional orthography.

I need not shield Drinkwater, because he will never read my book. So I have taken the liberty of making a special example of him, as far as that can be done without a phonetic alphabet, for the benefit of the mass of readers outside London who still form their notions of cockney dialect on Sam Weller. When I came to London in 1876, the Sam Weller dialect had passed away so completely that I should have given it up as a literary fiction if I had not discovered it surviving in a Middlesex village, and heard of it from an Essex one. Some time in the eighties the late Andrew Tuer called attention in the Pall Mall Gazette to several peculiarities of modern cockney, and to the obsolescence of the Dickens dialect that was still being copied from book to book by authors who never dreamt of using their ears, much less of training them to listen. Then came Mr. Anstey's cockney dialogues in Punch, a great advance, and Mr. Chevalier's coster songs and patter. The Tompkins verses contributed by Mr. Barry Pain to the London Daily Chronicle have also done something to bring the literary convention for cockney English up to date. But Tompkins sometimes perpetrates horrible solecisms. He will pronounce face as fits, accurately enough; but he will rhyme it quite impossibly to nice, which Tompkins would pronounce as newts: for example Mawl Enn Rowd for Mile End Road. This aw for i, which I have made Drinkwater use, is the latest stage of the old diphthongal oi, which Mr. Chevalier still uses. Irish, Scotch and north country readers must remember that Drinkwater's rs are absolutely unpronounced when they follow a vowel, though they modify the vowel very considerably. Thus, luggage is pronounced by him as laggige, but turn is not pronounced as tern, but as teun with the eu sounded as in French. The London r seems thoroughly understood in America, with the result, however, that the use of the r by Artemus Ward and other American dialect writers causes Irish people to misread them grotesquely. I once saw the pronunciation of malheureux represented in a cockney handbook by mal-err-err: not at all a bad makeshift to instruct a Londoner, but out of the question elsewhere in the British Isles. In America, representations of English speech dwell too derisively on the dropped or interpolated h. American writers have apparently not noticed the fact that the south English h is not the same as the never-dropped Irish and American h, and that to ridicule an Englishman for dropping it is as absurd as to ridicule the whole French and Italian nation for doing the same. The American h, helped out by a general agreement to pronounce wh as hw, is tempestuously audible, and cannot be dropped without being immediately missed. The London h is so comparatively quiet at all times, and so completely inaudible in wh, that it probably fell out of use simply by escaping the ears of children learning to speak. However that may be, it is kept alive only by the literate classes who are reminded constantly of its existence by seeing it on paper.

Roughly speaking, I should say that in England he who bothers about his hs is a fool, and he who ridicules a dropped h a snob. As to the interpolated h, my experience as a London vestryman has convinced me that it is often effective as a means of emphasis, and that the London language would be poorer without it. The objection to it is no more respectable than the objection of a street boy to a black man or to a lady in knickerbockers.

I have made only the most perfunctory attempt to represent the dialect of the missionary. There is no literary notation for the grave music of good Scotch.

BLACKDOWN,
   August 1900.

THE END